שַׁעֲרֵי תְּפִלָּה

THE GATES OF PRAYER

שַׁעֲרֵי תְּפִלָּה
THE GATES OF PRAYER

Services
for the
High Holy Days

by
Rabbi CHAIM STERN

illustrations by
Ezekiel Schloss

KTAV PUBLISHING HOUSE, INC.

SBN 87068-543-0

Manufactured in the United States of America

FOREWORD

This prayerbook was compiled to fill a need for High Holy Day Services which would be meaningful to young people.

I have attempted to sound the themes which are prominent on the Days of Awe. It is our hope that I have managed to do this with a directness of language and freshness of expression which will stimulate real worship rather than boredom or incomprehension.

This volume will be especially useful, I believe, because it offers more than the bare minimum of Services. There are two Services for Rosh Hashanah. Those who have need of one Service only therefore have a choice of Services, while those who need two can use both. In addition, there is a supplement which includes additional poems, prayers and songs.

I am grateful to my congregation, the members of Temple Beth-El of Northern Westchester, Chappaqua, New York, where these Services, in slightly different form, were first used. Their enthusiasm greatly heartened me, and inspired me to offer these Services to the general community.

And especially I thank, with love and affection, my wife Susan and my sons, whose creative suggestions and criticisms were extremely helpful, and whose confidence gives me courage.

Rabbi Chaim Stern

It is a very old folk tradition of our people that the world was created on Rosh Hashanah. So on this day we think about the world with special happiness. We give thanks for life, for all that is good and beautiful in creation.

ROSH HASHANAH SERVICE

I

READER

This is the New Year. Today we celebrate the birthday of the world. Although it is billions of years old, the world is always new and fresh when we see its beauty and look at it with happy eyes. Though there was a world long before we were born, we feel as if it were created especially for us when we think of God and thank him for it. And especially when we sing do we find ourselves saying on this day: "Happy birthday, world! Happy birthday, people! Many happy returns, plants and flowers, sun, moon and stars!" So let us sing a song now to the world. It tells the heavens to be glad, and the earth to sing for joy. It tells the sea and all its creatures to roar with happiness.

SONG

yis-m'chu ha-sha-ma-yim (3)	יִשְׂמְחוּ הַשָּׁמַיִם (3)
v'ta-gayl ha-a-retz.	וְתָגֵל הָאָרֶץ
yir-am ha-yam (3) u-m'lo-o	יִרְעַם הַיָּם (3) וּמְלוֹאוֹ
yir-am ha-yam (3) u-m'lo-o	יִרְעַם הַיָּם (3) וּמְלוֹאוֹ
yis-m'chu ha-sha-ma-yim (3)	יִשְׂמְחוּ הַשָּׁמַיִם (3)
v'ta-gayl ha-a-retz.	וְתָגֵל הָאָרֶץ

3

READER

This was a song of happiness, because we live in a wonderful world. How much more wonderful it could be if only we would try a little harder to make it so! We pray now that the coming year will be even better than last year. Let it be more peaceful, more joyous. Let all who had to go hungry last year, find food next year. May those who were cold be warm. May the lonely find many good friends. And may we often remember our God, who gave life to the world and who, although we cannot see or touch Him, speaks quietly inside our minds when we think of kindness and love. In a way, God is like the wind:

ALL READING

Who has seen the wind?
Neither I nor you;
But when the leaves hang trembling,
The wind is passing through.

READER

We do not see Him; He is like the wind;

ALL READING

Who has seen the wind?
Neither you nor I:
But when the trees bow down their heads
The wind is passing by.

READER

Passing through, passing by; yes, very like the wind:

ALL READING

Who has seen our God?
Neither you nor I;
But when our souls are singing,
Our God is passing by.
Who has seen our God?
Neither I nor you:
But when we hold each others' hearts,
Our God is passing through.

READER

We are glad to be together, as we are glad to be a part of God's singing world. We try, now, to feel a little closer to Him, to put Him into our minds and our hearts, so that in our love for God, we will love each other more deeply. With this as our hope, we turn to Him with words of praise:

ALL STANDING
READER

בָּרְכוּ אֶת־יְיָ הַמְבֹרָךְ:

Barechu et Adonai ha-m'vo-rach!

Praise the Lord, to whom all praise is due!

All READING, THEN ALL SINGING

בָּרוּךְ יְיָ הַמְבֹרָךְ לְעֹלָם וָעֶד:

Baruch Adonai ha-m'vo-rach l'olam va-ed!

We praise the Lord,
to whom all praise is due,
for ever and ever!

READER

We can do it the other way around, too; we can try to come closer to God by coming closer to people—to friends and neighbors, parents and teachers. We now remind ourselves that God is One. This means that every person is a child of God, so that all people are brothers to each other. We have not always been kind, we have not always been helpful. Now, as we prepare to say the *Shema,* we understand what it means—to love God is to try to help our brothers and sisters.

ALL READING, THEN ALL SINGING

שְׁמַע יִשְׂרָאֵל יְיָ אֱלֹהֵינוּ יְיָ אֶחָד:

Shema yisrael, Adonai elo-hay-nu, Adonai echad.

Hear, O Israel, the Lord is our God, the Lord is One.

בָּרוּךְ שֵׁם כְּבוֹד מַלְכוּתוֹ לְעוֹלָם וָעֶד:

Baruch shaym k'vod mal-chu-to l'olam va-ed.

We praise His name,
whose glorious kingdom is for ever and ever.

6

You shall love the Lord your God with all your heart,
  with all your soul,
  and with all your might.
Let these words,
  which I command you this day,
  be in your heart.
Teach them over and over again
  to your children;
  speak of them at home and away,
  morning, noon, and night.
Remember them,
  and do all my commandments:
  so shall you be holy to your God.

THE CONGREGATION WILL SIT

READER

Rosh Hashanah is a day with many names. One of these names is *yom ha-zikkaron*—the day of remembrance. We remember good days and bad, glad ones and sad. We remember the wrongs we have done, the promises we have kept, and those we did not keep. Why do we bother to remember? So that we may learn to do better in the year now beginning. Our best hope is that we may be able to do the things our Torah teaches us. These are the *mitzvot*, the commands of our religion:

ALL READING

"You shall love your neighbor
as yourself."

READER

"What is hateful to yourself, do not do to anyone else."

7

"Do justice,
love kindness
and walk humbly with your God."

READER

We might remember many other teachings today. But it may be enough for us to understand that the world is God's gift to us, the most precious of all gifts, not to be carelessly spoiled or thrown away. Let us take care of our bodies by keeping them clean and strong, helping them to grow; of our minds, by being eager to learn, and to understand what we learn; and of other people, by being cheerful, friendly, and helpful to them.

ALL READING

This is our hope for the New Year,
that we will remember God's gifts
and care for them:
our own bodies and minds,
our parents and our friends.

READER

Still we may not be wide-awake and alert enough to remember: so the sound of the ram's horn stirs us up. Now we cannot sleep, now we cannot forget. The *shofar* will awaken us, its voice will remind us. Three times we sound the call, as Jews have always done; three times we will remember our Jewish teachings. We stand now to thank God for his teachings of truth, as we hear the *shofar's* blast.

READER

Baruch atta Adonai,

   elohaynu melech ha-olam,

   asher kidd'shanu

   b'mitz-vo-tav

   v'tzi-vanu lish-mo-a kol shofar.

בָּרוּךְ אַתָּה יְיָ

אֱלֹהֵינוּ מֶלֶךְ הָעוֹלָם

אֲשֶׁר קִדְּשָׁנוּ

בְּמִצְוֹתָיו

וְצִוָּנוּ לִשְׁמוֹעַ קוֹל שׁוֹפָר:

ALL READING

We praise You,
Lord our God,
King of the universe,
for giving us Your commandments,
and for the sound of the shofar.

Amen.

READER

Baruch atta Adonai,

   elohaynu melech ha-olam,

   she-he-che-yanu

   v'ki-y'manu

   v'hi-gi-anu laz-man ha-zeh.

בָּרוּךְ אַתָּה יְיָ

אֱלֹהֵינוּ מֶלֶךְ הָעוֹלָם

שֶׁהֶחֱיָנוּ

וְקִיְּמָנוּ

וְהִגִּיעָנוּ לַזְּמַן הַזֶּה:

ALL READING

We praise You,
Lord our God,
King of the universe,
for giving us life,
caring for us,
and helping us to reach this holy day.

Amen.

READER

The *shofar* will be sounded three times. Let the first time remind us of the Jewish teaching of peace. The Torah says: "Nation shall not lift up sword against nation, and they shall study war no more." Let us not think only of nations. Let us be peaceful in our own lives as well. God, the world's true King, asks this of us.

(THE SHOFAR IS SOUNDED)

t'kiah;   תקיעה

   sh'varim/t'ru-ah;   שברים תרועה

      t'ki-ah.   תקיעה

Let the next notes remind us of the Jewish teaching of justice. The Torah says: "Justice, and only justice, shall you pursue." Nations must have justice, or the people cannot live. And let us remember to be just and fair in our own lives as well. God, the world's true Judge, asks this of us.

(THE SHOFAR IS SOUNDED)

t'ki-ah;   תקיעה

   sh'va-rim;   שברים

      t'ki-ah.   תקיעה

Let the last notes reminds us of the Jewish teaching of freedom. The Torah says: "Proclaim liberty throughout all the land, to all who live there." When our people escaped from slavery, they came to Mt. Sinai, and there promised to live by God's law. They knew that it is a law of freedom for all the world. May we, too, live by God's law, finding happiness and freedom all the days of our lives. God, the world's true Liberator, asks this of us.

(THE SHOFAR IS SOUNDED)

t'ki-ah;   תקיעה

  t'ru-ah;   תרועה

     t'ki-ah g'do-lah   תקיעה גדולה

THE CONGREGATION IS SEATED

READER

As we pledge ourselves to be loyal to God and to the Torah, to its teachings of peace, justice, and freedom; and as we hear the mystic sound of the *shofar* calling us to be true to our God and true to ourselves, our hearts sing a song of joyfulness and trust and nearness to God. Now we lift up our voices in a song of closeness. We attach ourselves to God; He belongs to us as we belong to Him.

CHOIR

We are Your people;	כִּי אָנוּ עַמֶּךָ
You are our King.	וְאַתָּה מַלְכֵּנוּ.
We are Your children;	אָנוּ בָנֶיךָ
You are our Father.	וְאַתָּה אָבִינוּ.
We are Your possession;	אָנוּ נַחֲלָתֶךָ
You are our Portion.	וְאַתָּה גוֹרָלֵנוּ.
We are Your flock;	אָנוּ צֹאנֶךָ
You are our Shepherd.	וְאַתָּה רוֹעֵנוּ.
We are Your vineyard;	אָנוּ כַרְמֶךָ
You are our Keeper.	וְאַתָּה נוֹטְרֵנוּ.
We are Your beloved;	אָנוּ רַעְיָתֶךָ
You are our Friend.	וְאַתָּה דוֹדֵנוּ.

SERVICE FOR THE READING OF THE TORAH

READER

The earth is the Lord's and all that is in it; the world and every living creature. Who may go up to the mountain of the Lord, and who may stand in his holy place? The one who does no wrong, and whose heart is pure.

Lord, who can say that he has done no wrong, and that his heart is pure? And yet we can say this: we have tried, and will try again, to live by the teachings of Your Torah. The more we grow in our knowledge and understanding of Your command-ments, the more we thank You, for they help us to live better lives.

THE CONGREGATION WILL STAND
AS SCROLL IS REMOVED FROM ARK

12

CHOIR

S'u sh'arim rashay-chem,

u-s'u pit-chay olam,

V'yavo melech ha'ka-vod.

Mi hu zeh melech ha-kavod?

Adonai tz'va-ot—

Hu melech ha-kavod. Selah!

שְׂאוּ שְׁעָרִים רָאשֵׁיכֶם.

וּשְׂאוּ פִּתְחֵי עוֹלָם.

וְיָבֹא מֶלֶךְ הַכָּבוֹד:

מִי הוּא זֶה מֶלֶךְ הַכָּבוֹד.

יְהֹוָה צְבָאוֹת.

הוּא מֶלֶךְ הַכָּבוֹד סֶלָה:

Lift up your heads, O gates,
And be lifted up, O ancient doors.
And let the King of Glory enter.
Who is the King of Glory?
The Lord of hosts—
He is the King of Glory!

READER

Now as we greet the Torah, we say again its most famous words. As Jews we live with these words in our hearts and our minds:

ALL READING, THEN SINGING

שְׁמַע יִשְׂרָאֵל יְהֹוָה אֱלֹהֵינוּ יְהֹוָה אֶחָד:

Shema yisrael, Adonai elo-hay-nu, Adonai echad.

Hear, O Israel, the Lord is our God, the Lord is One.

CHOIR

Lecha Adonai, ha-g'dulah v'ha-g'vurah לְךָ יְיָ הַגְּדֻלָּה וְהַגְּבוּרָה

v'ha-tiferet v'ha-naytzach v'ha-hod, וְהַתִּפְאֶרֶת וְהַנֵּצַח וְהַהוֹד,

ki chol ba-sha-mayim u-va-aretz. כִּי כֹל בַּשָּׁמַיִם וּבָאָרֶץ.

l'cha Adonai ha-mam-lacha לְךָ יְיָ הַמַּמְלָכָה

v'ha-mitnasay l'chol l'rosh. וְהַמִּתְנַשֵּׂא לְכֹל לְרֹאשׁ.

Yours, Lord, is greatness,
power, glory, victory and majesty.
Everything is Yours,
in heaven and earth.
Yours, Lord, is the kingdom;
You are supreme over all.

READER

בָּרְכוּ אֶת יְיָ הַמְבֹרָךְ:

Barechu et Adonai ha-m'vo-rach!

Praise the Lord, to whom all praise is due!

All READING

בָּרוּךְ יְיָ הַמְבֹרָךְ לְעוֹלָם וָעֶד:

Baruch Adonai ha-m'vo-rach l'olam va-ed!

We praise the Lord,
to whom all praise is due,
for ever and ever!

14

Baruch atta Adonai, בָּרוּךְ אַתָּה יְיָ

elohaynu melech ha-olam, אֱלֹהֵינוּ מֶלֶךְ הָעוֹלָם.

asher bachar banu אֲשֶׁר בָּחַר בָּנוּ

mikol ha-amim, מִכָּל הָעַמִּים

v'natan lanu et Torato. וְנָתַן לָנוּ אֶת תּוֹרָתוֹ.

Baruch atta Adonai, בָּרוּךְ אַתָּה יְיָ.

notayn ha-Torah. נוֹתֵן הַתּוֹרָה:

ALL READING

We praise You, O Lord our God,
King of the universe,
who have called us from among all peoples
by giving us the Torah.
We praise You, Lord,
Giver of the Torah.

Amen.

A. The Torah Reading
1. Based on Genesis 21:1-21.

Abraham and Sarah had become old, and Sarah had given up all hope of ever having a child. It was then that she became pregnant; and so, after Isaac was born, Sarah and Abraham knew the great joy which comes from being parents. They knew that this son was truly a gift from God, and to express their happiness, celebrated his birth with a joyful feast.

But now Sarah could see that there might be trouble in the future, because of the child which Abraham had already had by Hagar, Sarah's servant-woman. One day, therefore, with a heavy heart, Abraham gave provisions to Hagar and her child, Ishmael, and sent them elsewhere to live. Although this gave Abraham pain, he was comforted by God's promise that all would be well with them. Hagar was told that from her son would grow a great nation, even as a great nation, the people Israel, would come from Sarah's son Isaac. And so, while Abraham and his family dwelt in Canaan, which is now the land of Israel, Hagar and Ishmael settled to the south, in desert land, between Israel and Egypt.

2. Based on Genesis 22:1-18.

There came a day when Abraham was asked to live through the most difficult test that any man can be asked to undergo. One day, he seemed to hear God saying to him: "Take your son, your only son, whom you love so well, and offer him up to me as a sacrifice." Abraham asked no questions. He arose early the next morning. For three days, he traveled with Isaac to the place of the sacrifice. When they arrived they began their walk to the mountain where the sacrifice was to be made. Together they walked, father and son, the father knowing, the son suspecting, what was to be done. Neither one complained, as they went with perfect trust in God and in one another. If a terrible sadness lay upon Abraham's heart, it did not stop him from continuing to prepare for the deed which he was commanded to perform.

But human sacrifice was not a part of God's plan, and it was never intended that Abraham should take his son's life—only that he should learn to keep faith with God, and to understand that sometimes we are saved only when we take great risks. At such times Jews have always been inspired by Abraham's faith that God's love will see us through. At the last minute, God called to Abraham to tell him not to take his son's life. Instead, there in the bushes was a ram, caught in a thicket by its horns. This would be the fitting sacrifice, and Abraham's trust would be rewarded. The people Israel, his descendants and Isaac's, would be a great people, a blessing to the world. They would suffer many trials, but their faith would give them the strength to live through them, as it had given strength to Abraham.

READER

Baruch atta Adonai,   בָּרוּךְ אַתָּה יְיָ

elohaynu melech ha-olam,   אֱלֹהֵינוּ מֶלֶךְ הָעוֹלָם.

asher natan lanu Torat emet,   אֲשֶׁר נָתַן לָנוּ תּוֹרַת אֱמֶת.

v'cha-yay olam nata b'to-chaynu.   וְחַיֵּי עוֹלָם נָטַע בְּתוֹכֵנוּ.

Baruch atta Adonai,   בָּרוּךְ אַתָּה יְיָ.

notayn ha-Torah.   נוֹתֵן הַתּוֹרָה:

ALL READING

We praise You,
   O Lord our God, King of the universe,
   who have set eternal life within us
   by giving us a Torah of truth.
   We praise You, Lord,
   Giver of the Torah.

We praise You, Lord our God, King of the universe, for prophets of truth and justice. We praise You, Lord, the God of truth.

B. Haftarah

1. Based on I Samuel, 1:1-2:26.

There was a woman named Hannah, whose life was sad, for she had no children, although she was greatly loved by her husband. He tried to comfort her, but without success. Year after year she would go to the house of God to pray. It came to pass one year, at the temple, that Hannah wept bitterly and made a promise to God. If she had a son, she would bring him up to be a servant of God all the days of his life. Great was her joy when she learned, at the turn of the year, that her prayers had been answered and that she would have a child! The child was a son, and she named him Samuel, meaning, "God has heard me." She kept her promise. When the infant grew to childhood, she brought him to Shiloh, to the house of God. There he remained, to learn the service for which he was promised; and in her joy, Hannah sang a song of praise:

There is none holy as the Lord,
There is no God but You.
The Lord is a God of knowledge,
The Lord is a God of judgment.
He breaks the bows of the mighty,
He gives strength to those who were weak.
The woman who had no children,
Now will have many.
The Lord brings men low, and lifts them up.
He raises the weak from the dust,
And lifts the poor from the dirt.

He seats them next to princes,
And gives them a place of honor.

A glorious future was in store for the boy. For the man Samuel was later called to be prophet and judge, a great leader of his people.

2. Jeremiah 31:2-20.

This was Jeremiah's word to his people in a time of terrible trouble. The land had been invaded. Jerusalem had fallen. The Temple was destroyed. Jeremiah spoke in the name of God: Hear this message of hope, people of Israel. Even in the darkest time, when all seems lost, I, the Lord your God, am with you. My love for you will never die. Do not fear. You have repented of the evil things that you have done, and you will return to happiness. Your land will be yours once again. Your boys and girls will dance, your farmers will plant and enjoy the fruit. Laugh and be merry again. You will come from the ends of the earth, and your way will be smooth. You shall come with singing, and the land shall be like a well-watered garden. Your sadness will end.

I hear mother Rachel weeping—she, so loved by Jacob, who had so long to wait before being blessed with children, at last to have Joseph and Benjamin, only to die at Benjamin's birth: she weeps for her children—for all Israel. Weep no more, Rachel; wipe your eyes. Your future is bright with hope; the children are returning to their land. O Israel, says God, did you think I had forgotten you? Did you think your disgrace would last forever? No, you are my beloved child, I remember you fondly; my heart goes out to you, I will show you pity: this is God's promise.

THE CONGREGATION WILL STAND AS THE TORAH IS
BROUGHT FORWARD

READER

גַּדְּלוּ לַיָי אִתִּי . וּנְרוֹמְמָה שְׁמוֹ יַחְדָּו:

Gaddelu lAdonai iti, u-n'ro-m'mah shemo yach-dav.

O magnify the Lord with me,
and let us exalt His name together.

CHOIR

Hodo al eretz v'shamayim   הוֹדוֹ עַל אֶרֶץ וְשָׁמָיִם

va-yarem keren l'ammo,   וַיָּרֶם קֶרֶן לְעַמּוֹ

t'hillah l'chol chasidav,   תְּהִלָּה לְכָל חֲסִידָיו

liv-nay yisrael,   לִבְנֵי יִשְׂרָאֵל

am k'rovo.   עַם קְרֹבוֹ

Halleluyah!   הַלְלוּיָהּ:

His glory is over heaven and earth.
and He has raised His people high.
Let all who love Him praise Him.
Let the people Israel praise Him,
a people close to Him.
Praise the Lord!

20

READER

The law of the Lord is perfect, restoring the soul.

ALL READING

The teaching of the Lord is right,
rejoicing the heart.

READER

The commandment of the Lord is pure, enlightening the eyes.

ALL READING

The love of the Lord is strong,
lasting forever.

READER

A good teaching has been given you; keep it and live it. It is a tree of life to those who hold firmly to it, and those who cling to it are made happy. Its ways are ways of pleasantness, and all its paths are peace.

CHOIR

Etz chayyim hi	עֵץ חַיִּים הִיא
lammachazikim bah,	לַמַּחֲזִיקִים בָּהּ
v'tom'-chehah m'ushar.	וְתֹמְכֶיהָ מְאֻשָּׁר:
D'rachehah darchay noam,	דְּרָכֶיהָ דַרְכֵי נֹעַם
v'chol n'tivotehah	וְכָל נְתִיבוֹתֶיהָ
shalom.	שָׁלוֹם:
Hashivaynu Adonai	הֲשִׁיבֵנוּ יְיָ
aylecha v'nashuvah,	אֵלֶיךָ וְנָשׁוּבָה
chadaysh yamaynu k'kedem.	חַדֵּשׁ יָמֵינוּ כְּקֶדֶם:

THE ARK IS CLOSED

THE CONGREGATION WILL SIT

21

READER

Grant us peace, Your most precious gift, and help our people, Israel, to be messengers of peace to all the peoples of the world. Bless us, and all mankind, with a love of peace, and with the desire to bring an end to war and hatred. May every home be filled with health and happiness, and every heart be made peaceful, knowing of Your love. We praise You, Lord, Teacher of peace.

Now let us for a little while be very quiet. Let us hear only what our minds tell us, as we think about this day and about all we have learned about ourselves, our God, and the New Year.

SILENT MEDITATION

[This time is for your thoughts and feelings, your search for ways to bring yourself closer to God, and to become a better person during this new year.]

CHOIR

May the words of my mouth	יִהְיוּ לְרָצוֹן אִמְרֵי פִי
and the meditations of my heart	וְהֶגְיוֹן לִבִּי
be acceptable in Your sight,	לְפָנֶיךָ
O Lord, my Rock and my Redeemer.	יְיָ צוּרִי וְגוֹאֲלִי:
Amen.	אָמֵן.

THE CONGREGATION WILL STAND

ALL READING, OR ALL SINGING

Let us adore the ever-living God,
and render praise unto Him
Who spread out the heavens
and established the earth,
and whose glory
is revealed in the heavens above
and whose greatness
is manifest throughout the world.
He is our God and there is none else.

Va-anach-nu kor-im	וַאֲנַחְנוּ כֹּרְעִים
u-mish-ta-cha-vim u-mo-dim	וּמִשְׁתַּחֲוִים וּמוֹדִים
lif-nay melech	לִפְנֵי מֶלֶךְ
mal-chay ha-m'la-chim,	מַלְכֵי הַמְּלָכִים,
ha-ka-dosh baruch hu.	הַקָּדוֹשׁ, בָּרוּךְ הוּא.

23

READER

We bow the head in reverence, and worship the King of kings, the Holy One, praised be He.

Lord our God, we are thankful for this service, which has brought us together to think about You and Your law. We are grateful for this New Year, and pray that it will be a happier and more peaceful one than the year now ended. Especially do we thank You for Your many gifts to us—our own bodies and minds, the world we live in and its beauty, the Torah which enlightens our minds and teaches us how to live good lives and happy ones. We will remember the *shofar's* sound, and remain awake to its meaning.

ALL READING

Lord,

for the goodness of life
and for the power to make life sweet
and more beautiful,
we thank
and praise You.

READER

In days of old, our people imagined that everything we do is written in a heavenly book, the Book of Life, so they were careful to do things which they would be proud to see written in such a book. Then they greeted each other on the new year with these words: *L'shana tovah ti-ka-tayvu v'tay-cha-taymu*—"May you be written down and sealed for a good year." We, too, use this ancient greeting to each other, hoping that it will be a good year for all. And so we say:

ALL READING

לְשָׁנָה טוֹבָה תִּכָּתֵבוּ וְתֵחָתֵמוּ:

L'shana tovah ti-ka-tay-vu v'tay-cha-taymu.

May you be written down and sealed for a good year.

CLOSING SONG

Hi-nay ma-tov

u-ma na-im

shevet achim

gam ya-chad.

הִנֵּה מַה טּוֹב

וּמַה נָּעִים

שֶׁבֶת אַחִים

גַּם יָחַד.

How good it is,
  how pleasant,
  when brothers
  live together in unity.

CLOSING BLESSING

Rosh Hashanah is a day not for sadness but for hope. For this reason we eat an apple dipped in honey today. This custom speaks of our hope that the coming year will be a time of growing sweetness, and that we ourselves will learn ways of being sweeter in all that we say, in all that we do.

ROSH HASHANAH SERVICE

II

READER

Hope is a bird that sings
    through all my disappointments
        and helps me to smile at the world.

ALL READING

Hope is the bird that flies
    and carries my heart
        over days of sadness and hurt.

READER

Hope is a bird that sings
    even when the friend I trusted
        tells the secret he swore to keep.

ALL READING

Hope is the bird that flies
    even when I stand on the stage
        and have forgotten what comes next.

READER

Hope is a bird that sings
    even when I go to pay the cashier
        and find my pocket is empty.

ALL READING

Hope is the bird that flies
when I slam the door of the house
but leave the key inside.

READER

Hope is a bird that sings
even when I have told the truth
and they don't believe me.

ALL READING

Hope is the bird that flies
though I have offered a smile
and am answered by a frown.

READER

What is it that helps us to keep hoping? What brings the joy
back to our eyes? Deep down we know that troubles always end.

ALL READING

A new day comes, bringing fresh hope;
A new year comes, bringing happiness.

READER

And we know that we are loved. The love of our parents
never fails us. And God's love for us is always with us. We can
see it all through our lives, in the way our pains fade away, in
the clear sharp coolness of an autumn day, when we know how
good it is to be alive.

And if sometimes God's gentle touch we barely feel, then we
can reach for Him with song. Let us sing of our heart's desire
to hold Him closer:

SONG

Ay-leh chom-dah li-bi	אֵלֶּה חָמְדָה לִבִּי
chu-sah na v'al-na tit-a-laym	חוּסָה נָא וְאַלְנָא תִּתְעַלֵּם
Ay-leh chom-dah, chom-dah li-bi	אֵלֶּה חָמְדָה (2) לִבִּי
chu-sah na v'al-na tit-a-laym	חוּסָה נָא וְאַלְנָא תִּתְעַלֵּם
Ay-leh chom-dah, chom-dah li-bi	אֵלֶּה חָמְדָה (2) לִבִּי
chu-sah na v'al-na tit-a-laym.	חוּסָה נָא וְאַל תִּתְעַלֵּם

This is my deepest hope,
Have pity, don't go far away.

READER

There are many ways of bringing God closer to us. One way
is a very Jewish one: we grow closer to God by doing His commandments. It has been taught: There are some things which
we must never tire of doing; helping the poor, practicing love
and kindness, and studying Torah.

ALL READING

These are the things whose reward can never end:
  honoring father and mother,
  doing deeds of love and kindness,.
  being eager to learn,
  welcoming guests to our home,
  visiting the sick,
  comforting those in sorrow,
  praying sincerely,
  and making peace among people.

READER

But the study of Torah is equal to them all, because it teaches
us to do them all.

Lord be praised,
  King forever,
  for giving us minds which understand Your teachings.

Lord be praised,
  King forever,
  for hands that reach out to lift up those who fall.

Lord be praised,
  King forever,
  for ears that hear the cries of those who need help.

Lord be praised,
  King forever,
  for hearts that care about the needs of others.

Lord be praised,
  King forever,
  for eyes that see the beauty of earth and sky.

Lord be praised,
  King forever,
  for the new day and the new year.

READER

We give thanks and praise God for all that is good, true, and beautiful in our lives:

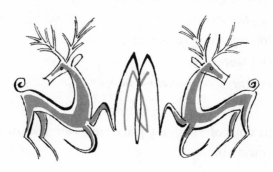

READER

בָּרְכוּ אֶת־יְיָ הַמְבֹרָךְ:

Barechu et Adonai ha-m'vo-rach!

Praise the Lord, to whom all praise is due!

ALL READING, THEN ALL SINGING

בָּרוּךְ יְיָ הַמְבֹרָךְ לְעוֹלָם וָעֶד:

Baruch Adonai ha-m'vo-rach l'olam va-ed!

We praise the Lord,
to whom all praise is due,
for ever and ever!

READER

Our God is One, the world is one world, and all its creatures
are God's children. We human beings belong to one family,
because there is a little bit of God in each one of us. Our people
has always known this to be true. Whenever we join in prayer,
we speak of it through the words of the *Shema.* May we always
treat one another as loving brothers and sisters. Let the words
of the *Shema* become so much a part of us, that we may live
them wherever we go and whatever we do.

ALL READING, THEN ALL SINGING

שְׁמַע יִשְׂרָאֵל יְיָ אֱלֹהֵינוּ יְיָ אֶחָד:

Shema yisrael, Adonai elo-hay-nu, Adonai echad.

Hear, O Israel, the Lord is our God, the Lord is One.

בָּרוּךְ שֵׁם כְּבוֹד מַלְכוּתוֹ לְעוֹלָם וָעֶד:

Baruch shaym k'vod mal-chu-to l'olam va-ed.

We praise His name,
whose glorious kingdom is for ever and ever.

ALL READING

You shall love the Lord your God with all your heart,
with all your soul,
and with all your might.
Let these words,
which I command you this day,
be in your heart.
Teach them over and over again
to your children;
speak of them at home and away,
morning, noon, and night.
Remember them,
and do all my commandments:
so shall you be holy to your God.

THE CONGREGATION WILL SIT

READER

On this day we look ahead and wonder what the next year will be like. We do not know everything about the days to come. But we do know the way in which we are taught to live. It has been taught:

ALL READING

"Greet all people with a friendly look."
This was the teaching of Shammai.

READER

"Be like Aaron, Moses' brother, who loved peace, followed the paths of peace, and cared for his fellow creatures." This was the teaching of Hillel.

ALL READING

Then we shall make this a good world,
as it has been taught:
"The world is preserved by three things:
by truth,
by justice,
and by peace."

READER

Long ago, our prophets taught that our people had a great work to do. We were to bring the light of God into the world, and to teach the world that God means justice and love, truth and knowledge. This we did. But there are times when, like all other people, we forget our own teachings. We do not always live by the truths we first gave to the world. And so Rosh Ha-shanah is called *Yom Teruah,* the day of the *shofar's* blast. By the sound of the ram's horn, we are awakened and reminded. When our people came together to meet God and to learn Torah at Mt. Sinai, they heard the *shofar's* call. In time of danger, the *shofar* would bring them running. Many times in the life of our people, it was the sound of the *shofar* which signaled to them to act. And still today, the horn wakes us up to the truth of our religion and tells us to remember not only to say true words, but to do true things. So now again, we hear the message of the ram's horn.

ALL STANDING
READER

Baruch atta Adonai,

elohaynu melech ha-olam,

asher kidd'shanu b'mitz-vo-tav

v'tzi-vanu lish-mo-a

kol shofar.

בָּרוּךְ אַתָּה יְיָ

אֱלֹהֵינוּ מֶלֶךְ הָעוֹלָם

אֲשֶׁר קִדְּשָׁנוּ בְּמִצְוֹתָיו

וְצִוָּנוּ לִשְׁמֹעַ

קוֹל שׁוֹפָר.

33

We praise You, Lord our God,
King of the universe,
for giving us Your commandments,
and for the sound of the shofar.

Amen.

READER

Baruch atta Adonai,	בָּרוּךְ אַתָּה יְיָ
elohaynu melech ha-olam,	אֱלֹהֵינוּ מֶלֶךְ הָעוֹלָם
she-he-che-yanu v'ki-y'manu	שֶׁהֶחֱיָנוּ וְקִיְּמָנוּ
v'hi-gi-anu laz-man ha-zeh.	וְהִגִּיעָנוּ לַזְּמַן הַזֶּה:

ALL READING

We praise You, Lord our God,
King of the universe,
for giving us life,
caring for us,
and helping us to reach this holy day.

Amen.

READER

The *shofar* will be sounded three times. Let its first call awaken us to the love of God, as it is written: "You shall love the Lord your God with all your heart, with all your soul, and with all your might." To love God is to be true to his teachings. When we love God and know that he is near, we make our lives happy and our hearts unafraid.

(THE SHOFAR IS SOUNDED)

t'kiah;	תקיעה
sh'varim/t'ru-ah;	שברים תרועה
t'ki-ah.	תקיעה

Let the second call of the *shofar* be a call which stirs us to a greater love of our people Israel. Of this it is written: "How good it is, and how pleasant, when brothers live together in unity." Our people has give the world many blessings. Still Israel lives, that more blessings may be our gift to the world. Happy are those who know that they are a part of a great, proud people. In good times they are joyful, in times of trouble they spring to help their brothers.

(THE SHOFAR IS SOUNDED)

t'ki-ah;   תקיעה

   sh'va-rim;   שברים

      t'ki-ah.   תקיעה

And the last notes signal our love for all the world. Our Torah asks: "Have we not all one Father? Has not One God created us all?" And the Torah commands: "You shall not wrong a stranger. You shall love him as yourself; for you were strangers in the land of Egypt." How great is our Torah, our teaching of love: love of God, love of our people, and love of the whole human race. Let the *shofar's* sound be with us this New Year's day to the next, that we may always be true to its meaning.

(THE SHOFAR IS SOUNDED)

t'ki-ah;   תקיעה

   t'ru-ah;   תרועה

      t'ki-ah g'do-lah   תקיעה גדולה

THE CONGREGATION IS SEATED

Our hearts are lifted high now, from the sound of the ancient
horn of the ram and from our knowledge of its meaning. Our
thoughts are of love and kindness and happiness. When we hold
such thoughts in our minds, when we are joyful and unafraid,
when we feel closer to each other, then we can be very sure that
God is with us right here, right now. He is in our feelings of
goodness and friendship, in our love and happiness. This is truly
God, even though we cannot see Him. Love makes us grow in
mind and soul, and the growing part is God whom we have
made a part of us. So let us sing a joyful song of Him.

ALL SINGING

There is none like our God,
  ayn kay-lo-hay-nu;   אֵין כֵּאלֹהֵינוּ,

There is none like our Lord,
  ayn ka-do-nay-nu.   אֵין כַּאדוֹנֵינוּ,

  Ayn kay-lo-hay-nu,   אֵין כֵּאלֹהֵינוּ,

  ayn ka-do-nay-nu,   אֵין כַּאדוֹנֵינוּ,

  Ayn k'mal-kay-nu,   אֵין כְּמַלְכֵּנוּ,

  ayn k'mo-shi-ay-nu.   אֵין כְּמוֹשִׁיעֵנוּ.

Who is like our God?
  mi chay-lo-hay-nu?   מִי כֵאלֹהֵינוּ,

Who is like our Lord?
  mi-cha-do-nay-nu?   מִי כַאדוֹנֵינוּ,

  Mi chay-lo-hay-nu,   מִי כֵאלֹהֵינוּ,

  mi cha-do-nay-nu,   מִי כַאדוֹנֵינוּ,

  Mi ch'mal-kay-nu,   מִי כְמַלְכֵּנוּ,

  mi ch'mo-shi-ay-nu.   מִי כְמוֹשִׁיעֵנוּ.

We will give thanks to our God, no-deh lay-lo-hay-nu.	נוֹדֶה לֵאלֹהֵינוּ,
We will give thanks to our Lord, no-deh la-do-nay-nu.	נוֹדֶה לַאדוֹנֵינוּ,
No-deh-lay-lo-hay-nu,	נוֹדֶה לֵאלֹהֵינוּ,
no-deh la-do-nay-nu.	נוֹדֶה לַאדוֹנֵינוּ,
No-deh l'mal-kay-nu,	נוֹדֶה לְמַלְכֵּנוּ,
no-deh l'mo-shi-ay-nu.	נוֹדֶה לְמוֹשִׁיעֵנוּ.
Blessed be our God, ba-ruch elo-hay-nu.	בָּרוּךְ אֱלֹהֵינוּ,
Blessed be our Lord, ba-ruch ado-nay-nu.	בָּרוּךְ אֲדוֹנֵינוּ,
Ba-ruch elo-hay-nu,	בָּרוּךְ אֱלֹהֵינוּ,
ba-ruch ado-nay-nu.	בָּרוּךְ אֲדוֹנֵינוּ,
Ba-ruch mal-kay-nu,	בָּרוּךְ מַלְכֵּנוּ,
ba-ruch mo-shi-ay-nu.	בָּרוּךְ מוֹשִׁיעֵנוּ.
You are our God, ata hu elo-hay-nu.	אַתָּה הוּא אֱלֹהֵינוּ,
You are our Lord, ata hu ado-nay-nu.	אַתָּה הוּא אֲדוֹנֵינוּ,
Ata hu elo-hay-nu,	אַתָּה הוּא אֱלֹהֵינוּ,
ata hu ado-nay-nu.	אַתָּה הוּא אֲדוֹנֵינוּ,
Ata hu mal-kay-nu,	אַתָּה הוּא מַלְכֵּנוּ,
ata hu mo-shi-ay-nu.	אַתָּה הוּא מוֹשִׁיעֵנוּ.

READER

And Moses spoke to Israel, saying: "Bring the people together —men, women and children, and the strangers who live in your cities—that they may hear, and learn to love the Lord your God, and to do faithfully every word of this Torah. And let the children, who do not yet know it, hear it and learn to love the Lord your God."

Ever since those words were said, our people has done this. We have come together to hear the words of Torah, to learn the ways of living which please God and make the hearts of mankind glad.

Once more, this very day, O God, Your children are ready to hear, to learn, to show their love for You by living better lives.

THE CONGREGATION WILL STAND

AS SCROLL IS REMOVED FROM ARK

CHOIR

s'u sh'arim rashay-chem,	שְׂאוּ שְׁעָרִים רָאשֵׁיכֶם
u-s'u pit-chay olam,	וּשְׂאוּ פִּתְחֵי עוֹלָם
v'yavo melech ha-kavod.	וְיָבֹא מֶלֶךְ הַכָּבוֹד.
mi hu zeh melech ha-kavod?	מִי הוּא זֶה מֶלֶךְ הַכָּבוֹד
Adonai tz'va-ot—	יְהֹוָה צְבָאוֹת
hu melech ha-kavod. Selah!	הוּא מֶלֶךְ הַכָּבוֹד סֶלָה.

Lift up your heads, O gates,
And be lifted up, O ancient doors,
And let the King of Glory enter.
Who is the King of Glory?
The Lord of hosts—
He is the King of Glory!

Now again we say, as we greet the Torah, its most famous words. As Jews we live with these words in our hearts and our minds:

ALL READING, THEN ALL SINGING

שְׁמַע יִשְׂרָאֵל יְהוָה אֱלֹהֵינוּ יְהוָה אֶחָד:

Shema yisrael, Adonai elohaynu, Adonai echad.

Hear, O Israel: the Lord is our God, the Lord is One.

CHOIR

Lecha Adonai, ha-g'dulah,	לְךָ יְיָ הַגְּדֻלָּה
v'ha-g'vurah v'ha-tiferet	וְהַגְּבוּרָה וְהַתִּפְאֶרֶת
v'ha-naytzach v'ha-hod,	וְהַנֵּצַח וְהַהוֹד,
ki-chol ba-sha-mayim u-va-aretz.	כִּי כֹל בַּשָּׁמַיִם וּבָאָרֶץ.
l'cha Adonai ha-mam-la cha,	לְךָ יְיָ הַמַּמְלָכָה
v'ha-mitnasay l'chol l'rosh.	וְהַמִּתְנַשֵּׂא לְכֹל לְרֹאשׁ.

Yours, Lord, is greatness,
  power, glory, victory, and majesty.
Everything is Yours,
  in heaven and earth.
Yours, Lord, is the kingdom;
You are supreme over all.

בָּרְכוּ אֶת יְיָ הַמְבֹרָךְ:

Barechu et Adonai   ha-m'vo-rach!

Praise the Lord, to whom all praise is due!

ALL READING

בָּרוּךְ יְיָ הַמְבֹרָךְ לְעוֹלָם וָעֶד:

Baruch Adonai ha-m'vo-rach l'o-lam va-ed!

We praise the Lord,
to whom all praise is due,
for ever and ever!

READER

Baruch atta Adonai,	בָּרוּךְ אַתָּה יְיָ
elohaynu melech ha-olam,	אֱלֹהֵינוּ מֶלֶךְ הָעוֹלָם.
asher bachar banu	אֲשֶׁר בָּחַר בָּנוּ
mikol ha-amim,	מִכָּל הָעַמִּים
v'natan lanu et Torato.	וְנָתַן לָנוּ אֶת תּוֹרָתוֹ.
Baruch atta Adonai,	בָּרוּךְ אַתָּה יְיָ.
notayn ha-Torah.	נוֹתֵן הַתּוֹרָה.

ALL READING

We praise You, O Lord our God,
King of the universe,
who have called us from among all peoples
by giving us the Torah.
We praise You, Lord,
Giver of the Torah.

Amen.

THE CONGREGATION WILL SIT FOR THE READING OF THE TORAH

TORAH AND HAFTARAH READINGS

A. The Torah Reading
1. Based on Genesis 21:1-21.

Abraham and Sarah had become old, and Sarah had given up all hope of ever having a child. It was then that she became pregnant; and so, after Isaac was born, Sarah and Abraham knew the great joy which comes from being parents. They knew that this son was truly a gift from God, and to express their happiness, celebrated his birth with a joyful feast.

But now Sarah could see that there might be trouble in the future, because of the child which Abraham had already had by Hagar, Sarah's servant-woman. One day, therefore, with a heavy heart, Abraham gave provisions to Hagar and her child, Ishmael, and sent them elsewhere to live. Although this gave Abraham pain, he was comforted by God's promise that all would be well with them. Hagar was told that from her son would grow a great nation, even as a great nation, the people Israel, would come from Sarah's son Isaac. And so, while Abraham and his family dwelt in Canaan, which is now the land of Israel, Hagar and Ishmael settled to the south, in desert land, between Israel and Egypt.

2. Based on Genesis 22:1-18.

There came a day when Abraham was asked to live through the most difficult test that any man can be asked to undergo. One day, he seemed to hear God saying to him: "Take your son, your only son, whom you love so well, and offer him up to me as a sacrifice." Abraham asked no questions. He arose early the next morning. For three days, he traveled with Isaac to the place of the sacrifice. When they arrived they began their walk to the mountain where the sacrifice was to be made. Together they walked, father and son, the father knowing, the son suspecting, what was to be done. Neither one complained, as they went with

41

perfect trust in God and in one another. If a terrible sadness lay upon Abraham's heart, it did not stop him from continuing to prepare for the deed which he was commanded to perform.

But human sacrifice was not a part of God's plan, and it was never intended that Abraham should take his son's life—only that he should learn to keep faith with God, and to understand that sometimes we are saved only when we take great risks. At such times Jews have always been inspired by Abraham's faith that God's love will see us through. At the last minute, God called to Abraham to tell him not to take his son's life. Instead, there in the bushes was a ram, caught in a thicket by its horns. This would be the fitting sacrifice, and Abraham's trust would be rewarded. The people Israel, his descendants and Isaac's, would be a great people, a blessing to the world. They would suffer many trials, but their faith would give them the strength to live through them, as it had given strength to Abraham.

READING OF THE TORAH
READER

Baruch atta Adonai,	בָּרוּךְ אַתָּה יְיָ
elohaynu melech ha-olam,	אֱלֹהֵינוּ מֶלֶךְ הָעוֹלָם.
asher natan lanu Torat emet,	אֲשֶׁר נָתַן לָנוּ תּוֹרַת אֱמֶת.
v'cha-yay olam nata b'to-chaynu.	וְחַיֵּי עוֹלָם נָטַע בְּתוֹכֵנוּ.
Baruch atta Adonai,	בָּרוּךְ אַתָּה יְיָ.
notayn ha-Torah.	נוֹתֵן הַתּוֹרָה:

We praise You,
O Lord our God, King of the universe,
who have set eternal life within us
by giving us a Torah of truth.
We praise You, Lord,
Giver of the Torah.

BLESSING BEFORE THE HAFTARAH

We praise You, Lord our God, King of the universe, for prophets of truth and justice. We praise You, Lord, the God of truth.

B. Haftarah

1. Based on I Samuel, 1:1-2:26.

There was a woman named Hannah, whose life was sad, for she had no children, although she was greatly loved by her husband. He tried to comfort her, but without success. Year after year she would go to the house of God to pray. It came to pass one year, at the temple, that Hannah wept bitterly and made a promise to God. If she had a son, she would bring him up to be a servant of God all the days of his life. Great was her joy when she learned, at the turn of the year, that her prayers had been answered and that she would have a child! The child was a son, and she named him Samuel, meaning, "God has heard me." She kept her promise. When the infant grew to childhood, she brought him to Shiloh, to the house of God. There he remained, to learn the service for which he was promised; and in her joy, Hannah sang a song of praise:

There is none holy as the Lord,
There is no God but You.
The Lord is a God of knowledge,
The Lord is a God of judgment.
He breaks the bows of the mighty,
He gives strength to those who were weak.
The woman who had no children,
Now will have many.
The Lord brings men low, and lifts them up.
He raises the weak from the dust,
And lifts the poor from the dirt.
He seats them next to princes,
And gives them a place of honor.

A glorious future was in store for the boy. For the man Samuel was later called to be prophet and judge, a great leader of his people.

2. Jeremiah 31:2-20.

This was Jeremiah's word to his people in a time of terrible trouble. The land had been invaded. Jerusalem had fallen. The Temple was destroyed. Jeremiah spoke in the name of God: Hear this message of hope, people of Israel. Even in the darkest time, when all seems lost, I, the Lord your God, am with you. My love for you will never die. Do not fear. You have repented of the evil things that you have done, and you will return to happiness. Your land will be yours once again. Your boys and girls will dance, your farmers will plant, and enjoy the fruit. Laugh and be merry again. You will come from the ends of the earth, and your way will be smooth. You shall come with singing, and the land shall be like a well-watered garden. Your sadness will end.

I hear mother Rachel weeping—she, so loved by Jacob, who had so long to wait before being blessed with children, at last to have Joseph and Benjamin, only to die at Benjamin's birth: she weeps for her children—for all Israel. Weep no more, Rachel; wipe your eyes. Your future is bright with hope; the children are returning to their land. O Israel, says God, did you think I had forgotten you? Did you think your disgrace would last forever? No, you are my beloved child, I remember you fondly; my heart goes out to you, I will show you pity: this is God's promise.

READER

גַּדְּלוּ לַיָי אִתִּי . וּנְרוֹמְמָה שְׁמוֹ יַחְדָּו:

Gaddelu l'Adonai iti, u-n'ro-m'mah shemo yach-dav.

O magnify the Lord with me,
    and let us exalt His name together.

CHOIR

Hodo al eretz v'shamayim	הוֹדוֹ עַל אֶרֶץ וְשָׁמָיִם
va-yarem keren l'ammo,	וַיָרֶם קֶרֶן לְעַמּוֹ
t'hillah l'chol chasidav,	תְּהִלָּה לְכָל חֲסִידָיו
liv-nay yisrael,	לִבְנֵי יִשְׂרָאֵל
am k'rovo.	עַם קְרֹבוֹ
Halleluyah!	הַלְלוּיָה.

*His glory is over heaven and earth.
and He has raised His people high.
Let all who love Him praise Him.
Let the people Israel praise Him,
a people close to Him.
Praise the Lord!*

READER
Happy are those who search for wisdom.

ALL READING
And those who find understanding.

READER
Its fruits are sweet, better than silver or fine gold.

46

ALL READING

It is more precious than rubies;
there is no treasure like Torah.

READER

It is a tree of life to those who hold firmly to it, and those who
cling to it are made happy. Its ways are ways of pleasantness, and
all its paths are peace.

CHOIR

Etz chayyim hi	עֵץ חַיִּים הִיא
lammachazikim bah,	לַמַּחֲזִיקִים בָּהּ
v'tom'-chehah m'ushar.	וְתֹמְכֶיהָ מְאֻשָּׁר:
D'rachehah darchay noam,	דְּרָכֶיהָ דַרְכֵי נֹעַם
v'chol n'tivotehah shalom.	וְכָל נְתִיבוֹתֶיהָ
	שָׁלוֹם:
Hashivaynu Adonai	הֲשִׁיבֵנוּ יְיָ
aylecha v'nashuvah,	אֵלֶיךָ וְנָשׁוּבָה
chadaysh yamaynu k'kedem.	חַדֵּשׁ יָמֵינוּ כְּקֶדֶם:

THE ARK IS CLOSED
THE CONGREGATION WILL SIT
READER

Lord, we have learned through the study of Your Torah and
through the history of our people many shining truths. May we
never forget how good the world is, and how sweet is the taste
of freedom. We know that our life and its goodness is the gift
of loving parents and kind friends. And we know that their love
and kindness are gifts from You, who are the Creator of all things.

ALL READING

Because we know all this, we know too that You created us, Your children, to live in peace and friendship all over the world. O let us all be filled with the spirit of wisdom and justice, love and mercy, that we may learn to make this a peaceful world. Then will there be enough for us all. No more shall any child go hungry, or any man be afraid, or any mother cry for her children lost in war. We praise You, Lord, Teacher of peace.

READER

Now let us for a little while be very quiet. Let us hear only what our minds tell us, as we think about this day and of all that we have learned about ourselves, our God and the new year.

SILENT MEDITATION

[This time is for your thoughts and feelings, your search for ways to bring yourself closer to God, and to become a better person during this new year.]

May the words of my mouth	יִהְיוּ לְרָצוֹן אִמְרֵי פִי
and the meditations of my heart	וְהֶגְיוֹן לִבִּי
be acceptable in Your sight,	לְפָנֶיךָ
O Lord,	יְיָ
my Rock and my Redeemer.	צוּרִי וְגוֹאֲלִי:
Amen.	אָמֵן

48

ALL READING, OR ALL SINGING

Let us adore the ever-living God,
and render praise unto Him
Who spread out the heavens
and established the earth,
and whose glory
is revealed in the heavens above
and whose greatness
is manifest throughout the world.
He is our God and there is none else.

Va-anach-nu kor-im   וַאֲנַחְנוּ כֹּרְעִים

u-mish-ta-cha-vim u-mo-dim   וּמִשְׁתַּחֲוִים וּמוֹדִים

lif-nay melech   לִפְנֵי מֶלֶךְ

mal-chay ha-m'la-chim,   מַלְכֵי הַמְּלָכִים,

ha-ka-dosh baruch hu.   הַקָּדוֹשׁ, בָּרוּךְ הוּא.

READER

We bow the head in reverence, and worship the King of kings, the Holy One, praised be He.

Lord our God, we thank You for this new year, and for the hope it brings us. We hope for a happy year for ourselves and our families, for all the members of this congregation, and for our people Israel. May it be a year of happiness for us, a year for doing many good things, a year for learning more and more about Your world. And may this year be good for all people everywhere, bringing peace instead of war, and freedom and justice wherever these are not found today.

May there be more love and less hatred, more people helping each other, and less sickness and sorrow. With these hopes and prayers for the New Year, we say to each other the old greeting: *l'shana tovah ti-ka-tay-vu-v'tay-cha-tay-mu*—"May you be written down and sealed for a good year."

ALL READING

לְשָׁנָה טוֹבָה תִּכָּתֵבוּ וְתֵחָתֵמוּ:

L'shana tovah ti-ka-tay-vu v'tay-cha-taymu.

*"May you be written down
and sealed for a good year."*

CLOSING SONG

Shalom cha-vay-rim.

   Shalom cha-vay-rim,

   Shalom, shalom.

   L'hit-ra-ot, l'hit-ra-ot,

   Shalom, shalom.

שָׁלוֹם חֲבֵרִים,

שָׁלוֹם חֲבֵרִים,

שָׁלוֹם, שָׁלוֹם.

לְהִתְרָאוֹת, לְהִתְרָאוֹת,

שָׁלוֹם, שָׁלוֹם.

Our hope is for peace,
   Our prayer is for peace,
   Shalom, shalom.
   Let all men be friends,
   Let all men be free,
   Shalom, shalom.

Shalom cha-vay-rim.	שָׁלוֹם חֲבֵרִים,
Shalom cha-vay rim,	שָׁלוֹם חֲבֵרִים,
Shalom, shalom.	שָׁלוֹם, שָׁלוֹם.
L'hit-ra-ot, l'hit-ra-ot,	לְהִתְרָאוֹת, לְהִתְרָאוֹת,
Shalom, shalom.	שָׁלוֹם, שָׁלוֹם.

CLOSING BLESSING

One of the beautiful customs of our people is the practice of asking one another's forgiveness for any wrong or hurt that may have been done during the past year. This we do just before Yom Kippur, because we can ask God's forgiveness only after we have forgiven and been forgiven by other people. So let us begin this service by turning to our friends and neighbors and giving them the hand of pardon and friendship. Then we shall be ready to turn to God with peaceful hearts.

YOM KIPPUR SERVICE

READER
This is Yom Kippur, the Day of Atonement. To "atone" means to become "at one" with God. We can come closer to God by thinking about him, by understanding that the world he has made is very precious, and by loving other people—our family and friends, our classmates and our neighbors. On this day, when we remember our wrongdoings of the past year, we feel deeply sorry. In all our prayers, our thoughts, and our songs, we say: "I will try very hard to be a more loving and helpful person next year."

We will try very hard.
We will learn to love and always to have
a cheerful word for others.
We will try to grow in goodness, and in learning,
To forgive those who wrong us,
and to do no wrong to any one of God's children.

READER

We seek today to come closer to God. We have learned that God is wherever we are, even though we cannot see Him. Where can we find Him?

ALL READING

We find Him in the loveliness of flowers,
In the refreshing spray of showers.

READER

We find Him in the law that tells the far-off stars to shine;
And in the wondrous story of our people, there too we see Him.
We find Him when we sing songs of celebration and prayer.
Let us sing such a song now, a song which prays that we may
    never lose this good and lovely world.

ALL SINGING

Eli, Eli	אֵלִי אֵלִי,
shelo yi-ga-mer l'olam,	שֶׁלֹּא יִגָּמֵר לְעוֹלָם
ha-chol v'ha-yam,	הַחוֹל וְהַיָּם,
rish-rush shel ha-ma-yim,	רִשְׁרוּשׁ שֶׁל הַמַּיִם,
b'rak ha-sha-ma-yim,	בְּרַק הַשָּׁמַיִם,
t'fi-lat ha-a-dam.	תְּפִלַּת הָאָדָם.
ha-chol v'ha-yam,	הַחוֹל וְהַיָּם,

rish-rush shel ha-ma-yim,

b'rak ha-sha-ma-yim,

t'fi-lat ha-a-dam.

רִשְׁרוּשׁ שֶׁל הַמַּיִם,

בְּרַק הַשָּׁמַיִם,

תְּפִלַּת הָאָדָם.

O Lord, my God,
 I pray that these things never end:
The sand and the sea,
The rush of the waters,
The crash of the heavens,
The prayer of man.
The sand and the sea,
The rush of the waters,
The crash of the heavens,
The prayer of man.

READER

The world is large and beautiful. But our teachers remind us that one small hand before our eyes can shut the world away from our sight. Sometimes, too, it seems as if God is shut away from us. But as the world is with us even when we do not see it, so is God with us, even when we cannot feel Him.

ALL READING

He is with all those who think they are lost:
the poor and lonely, the sad and the sick.

READER

We find Him in words of truth, and in all those who live and speak truth and gentleness.

ALL READING

He is in all things old and new;
We see Him in the play of children
 and the smiles of parents.

READER

And His voice is the sound of song. Today we shall hear a very special song, called *Kol Nidre.* It means "All Promises"— reminding us of the promises we made last year. If we were not able to keep some of them, we ask to be forgiven. Even more than the words, we hear the melody, and it is a sad one—beautiful but sad. Life has often been sad for our people. There have been some who tried to save their lives by pretending they were not Jews. Secretly, they continued to be loyal to God and to their people. Then there came a day when they were able to return to us. They came out of hiding and, on the eve of Yom Kippur, the *Kol Nidre* had a special meaning for them. As they listened to its words and its melody, they begged to be forgiven for the promises they had not been able to keep. So *Kol Nidre* is sad, and beautiful. Sad, because it reminds us that our people has suffered so much. Beautiful, because our people is alive, and will always live, while there are Jews with courage and faith.

As we take the Torah out of the Ark and hold it while we hear the *Kol Nidre,* we are reminded of our own promises: to live by the Torah, our tree of life, and always to be loyal to our God and our people.

**ALL STAND AS THE TORAH IS TAKEN FROM THE ARK
AND THE KOL NIDRE IS SUNG**

כָּל נִדְרֵי. וֶאֱסָרֵי. וַחֲרָמֵי. וְקוֹנָמֵי. וְכִנּוּיֵי. וְקִנּוּסֵי.
וּשְׁבוּעוֹת. דִּנְדַרְנָא. וּדְאִשְׁתְּבַעְנָא. וּדְאַחֲרִימְנָא. וְדַאֲסָרְנָא
עַל נַפְשָׁתָנָא. מִיּוֹם כִּפֻּרִים זֶה עַד יוֹם כִּפֻּרִים הַבָּא
עָלֵינוּ לְטוֹבָה. כֻּלְּהוֹן אִחֲרַטְנָא בְהוֹן. כֻּלְּהוֹן יְהוֹן שָׁרָן.
שְׁבִיקִין. שְׁבִיתִין. בְּטֵלִין וּמְבֻטָּלִין. לָא שְׁרִירִין וְלָא
קַיָּמִין: נִדְרָנָא לָא נִדְרֵי. וֶאֱסָרָנָא לָא אֱסָרֵי. וּשְׁבוּעָתָנָא
לָא שְׁבוּעוֹת:

56

O God, we will do our best to keep every promise, fulfill every good intention and every resolution that we make during the year that has just begun, from this Day of Atonement to the next Day of Atonement. But if there are promises that we truly cannot keep, however hard we try, we pray that we may be forgiven. And we ask pardon, too, for those promises we could not keep in the year now ended. Now and always, we ask forgiveness, as we remember the words of Your Torah: "The Lord said, 'I have pardoned as you have asked.' "

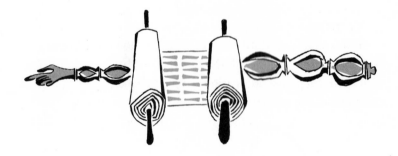

READER

We have heard the words and melody of the *Kol Nidre,* and we have learned something of its story, which teaches us that God has been with our people through all our days and years. He has given us hope in times of trouble, happiness in times of freedom. Happy or sad, we have always looked with love to our God. Today, still, we look to Him with love and call out words of praise:

בָּרְכוּ אֶת יְיָ הַמְבֹרָךְ:

Barechu et Adonai ha-m'vo-rach!

Praise the Lord, to whom all praise is due!

All READING, THEN ALL SINGING

בָּרוּךְ יְיָ הַמְבֹרָךְ לְעוֹלָם וָעֶד:

Baruch Adonai ha-m'vo-rach l'olam va-ed!

We praise the Lord,
to whom all praise is due,
for ever and ever!

READER

We praise the God whom we know as One, and whose children are one family. Black and white, yellow and brown, tall and lean, small and round, long-haired and bald, from all continents, all religions, all nations and languages—all are God's children, all are *one.* We have a very old and short way of saying this—and we say it together in words that come from the Torah:

ALL READING

שְׁמַע יִשְׂרָאֵל יְהֹוָה אֱלֹהֵינוּ יְהֹוָה אֶחָד:

Shema yisrael, Adonai elohaynu, Adonai echad.

Hear, O Israel, the Lord is our God, the Lord is One.

בָּרוּךְ שֵׁם כְּבוֹד מַלְכוּתוֹ לְעוֹלָם וָעֶד:

Baruch shaym k'vod mal-chu-to l'olam va-ed.

We praise His name, whose glorious kingdom
is forever and ever.

You shall love the Lord your God
with all your heart,
with all your soul,
and with all your might. Let these words,
which I command you this day,
be in your heart.
Teach them
over and over again
to your children;
speak of them
at home and away,
morning,
noon
and night. Remember them,
and do all My commandments;
so shall you be holy to your God.

THE TORAH IS RETURNED TO THE ARK
AND THE CONGREGATION IS SEATED

READER

Today we think of what we would like to be. We begin with our faults—our mistakes and wrongdoings of the past year still remain in our minds. But now, on this holy day, this day of truth, we say: we are sorry, we are truly sorry, and hope to do better. We have a prayer for this, called *Al Chet: al chet shecha-tanu*—for the wrong we have done, we are truly sorry.

ALL READING

Al chet she-cha-ta-nu—

עַל חֵטְא שֶׁחָטָאנוּ

for the wrong we have done,
we are truly sorry.

READER

for the wrong we have done,
for not always speaking the truth,
we are sorry.

ALL READING

Al chet she-cha-ta-nu—

עַל חֵטְא שֶׁחָטָאנוּ

for having been stubborn or lazy,
we are sorry.

READER

for the wrong we have done,
for having hurt other people's feelings,
we are sorry.

ALL READING

Al chet she-cha-ta-nu—

עַל חֵטְא שֶׁחָטָאנוּ

for having been unfair or spiteful,
we are sorry.

READER

for the wrong we have done,
for having spoken when we should have been listening,
we are sorry.

ALL READING

Al chet she-cha-ta-nu—

עַל חֵטְא שֶׁחָטָאנוּ

for having remained silent when we should have
*   spoken up,*
we are sorry.

for the wrong we have done,
for having been jealous of other people's luck,
we are sorry.

ALL READING

Al chet she-cha-ta-nu— עַל חֵטְא שֶׁחָטָאנוּ

for anger or bad temper,
for times when we might have been cheerful
but were bitter instead,
we are sorry.

READER

for the wrong we have done,
for the times when we failed to honor our parents,
we are sorry.

ALL READING

Al chet she-cha-ta-nu— עַל חֵטְא שֶׁחָטָאנוּ

for the times when we failed to honor our teachers,
we are sorry.

READER

for the wrong we have done,
for all these things,
O God of forgiveness,
pardon and forgive us.

CHOIR

V'al kulam, elo-ah s'lichot, וְעַל כֻּלָּם אֱלוֹהַּ סְלִיחוֹת

s'lach lanu, סְלַח לָנוּ

m'chal lanu, מְחַל לָנוּ

ca-per lanu. כַּפֶּר לָנוּ.

READER

What does being sorry really mean? It is written:
Three things there are that will never come back:
The arrow shot forth on its destined track;
The appointed hour that could not wait;
And the helpful word that was spoken too late.

ALL READING

This means that what we have done is done.
We cannot change the words we have spoken,
and we cannot speak
after the time for speaking is done.
We cannot bring back the time
when we should have helped but did not.

READER

What then can we do? Why do we say we are sorry?

ALL READING

Not because of what has been done
but because of what we will do next year.
We will try to learn from our mistakes
so that we may do the right thing
at the right time in the year ahead.

READER

How should we live in the year to come? These are the words
of gentle Hillel: "If I am not for myself, who will be for me?"

ALL READING

We cannot live only for others.
We must live for ourselves as well.

READER

And Hillel continued: "But if I am for myself only, what
am I?"

What sort of person lives only for himself?
Partly for ourselves and partly for others—
this is the way we should live.

READER
And Hillel ended: "And if not now, when?"

ALL READING
Now—at every moment,
is the time to live the right way.
We must not wait for another time
to live by the teachings of the Torah,
to live as God wants us to live.
The time is always now.

READER
Yes, the time is now, to live as we have learned:

ALL READING
"You shall love your neighbor
as yourself."

READER
"What is hateful to yourself, do not do to anyone else."

ALL READING
"Do justice,
love kindness
and walk humbly with your God."

READER
At the beginning of our ten days of repentance, we heard the sound of the *shofar*. It was a voice teaching us to love peace, justice and freedom. We will remember this today, and all the days of this year.

ALL READING

O God, we will give thanks
for all Your gifts to us.
We will learn to care for Your world,
for our own bodies and minds,
and for the people around us.
Our days will be bright
with good cheer, friendship and
helpfulness. Our good intentions
will be followed by good deeds.

READER

We will turn to You, Lord our God, and sing a song of love
and friendship.

CHOIR

We are Your people;	כִּי אָנוּ עַמֶּךָ
You are our King.	וְאַתָּה מַלְכֵּנוּ.
We are Your children;	אָנוּ בָנֶיךָ
You are our Father.	וְאַתָּה אָבִינוּ.
We are Your possession;	אָנוּ נַחֲלָתֶךָ
You are our Portion.	וְאַתָּה גוֹרָלֵנוּ.
We are Your flock;	אָנוּ צֹאנֶךָ
You are our Shepherd.	וְאַתָּה רוֹעֵנוּ.
We are Your vineyard;	אָנוּ כַרְמֶךָ
You are our Keeper.	וְאַתָּה נוֹטְרֵנוּ.
We are Your beloved;	אָנוּ רַעְיָתֶךָ
You are our Friend.	וְאַתָּה דוֹדֵנוּ.

READER

And Moses spoke to Israel, saying: "Bring the people together
—men, women and children, and the strangers who live in your
cities—that they may hear, and learn to love the Lord your God,
and to do faithfully every word of this Torah. And let the children, who do not yet know it, hear it and learn to love the Lord
your God."

Ever since those words were said, our people has done this.
We have come together to hear the words of Torah, to learn the
ways of living which please God and make the hearts of mankind glad.

Once more, this very day, O God, Your children are ready to
hear, to learn, to show their love for You by living better lives.

THE CONGREGATION WILL STAND

AS SCROLL IS REMOVED FROM ARK

CHOIR

s'u sh'arim rashay-chem,	שְׂאוּ שְׁעָרִים רָאשֵׁיכֶם
u-s'u pit-chay olam,	וּשְׂאוּ פִּתְחֵי עוֹלָם
v'yavo melech ha-kavod.	וְיָבֹא מֶלֶךְ הַכָּבוֹד.
mi hu zeh melech ha-kavod?	מִי הוּא זֶה מֶלֶךְ הַכָּבוֹד
Adonai tz'va-ot—	יְהֹוָה צְבָאוֹת
hu melech ha-kavod. Selah!	הוּא מֶלֶךְ הַכָּבוֹד סֶלָה.

Lift up your heads, O gates,
And be lifted up, O ancient doors,
And let the King of Glory enter.
Who is the King of Glory?
The Lord of hosts—
He is the King of Glory!

READER

Now again we say, as we greet the Torah, its most famous
words. As Jews we live with these words in our hearts and our
minds:

65

ALL READING, THEN ALL SINGING

שְׁמַע יִשְׂרָאֵל יְהֹוָה אֱלֹהֵינוּ יְהֹוָה אֶחָד.

Shema yisrael, Adonai elohaynu, Adonai echad.

Hear, O Israel: the Lord is our God, the Lord is One.

CHOIR

Lecha Adonai, ha-g'dulah v'ha-g'vurah לְךָ יְיָ הַגְּדֻלָּה וְהַגְּבוּרָה

v'ha-tiferet v'ha-naytzach v'ha-hod, וְהַתִּפְאֶרֶת וְהַנֵּצַח וְהַהוֹד,

ki chol ba-sha-mayim u-va-aretz. כִּי כֹל בַּשָּׁמַיִם וּבָאָרֶץ.

l'cha Adonai ha-mam-lacha לְךָ יְיָ הַמַּמְלָכָה

v'ha-mitnasay l'chol i'rosh. וְהַמִּתְנַשֵּׂא לְכֹל לְרֹאשׁ.

Yours, Lord, is greatness,
   power, glory, victory, and majesty.
Everything is Yours,
   in heaven and earth.
Yours, Lord, is the kingdom;
You are supreme over all.

READER

בָּרְכוּ אֶת־יְיָ הַמְבֹרָךְ:

Barechu et Adonai   ha-m'vo-rach!

Praise the Lord, to whom all praise is due!

ALL READING

בָּרוּךְ יְיָ הַמְבֹרָךְ לְעוֹלָם וָעֶד:

Baruch Adonai ha-m'vo-rach l'o-lam va-ed!

We praise the Lord,
   to whom all praise is due,
   for ever and ever!

READER

Baruch atta Adonai,	בָּרוּךְ אַתָּה יְיָ
elohaynu melech ha-olam,	אֱלֹהֵינוּ מֶלֶךְ הָעוֹלָם.
asher bachar banu	אֲשֶׁר בָּחַר בָּנוּ
mikol ha-amim,	מִכָּל הָעַמִּים
v'natan lanu et Torato.	וְנָתַן לָנוּ אֶת תּוֹרָתוֹ.
Baruch atta Adonai,	בָּרוּךְ אַתָּה יְיָ.
notayn ha-Torah.	נוֹתֵן הַתּוֹרָה.

ALL READING

We praise You, O Lord our God,
King of the universe,
who have called us from among all peoples
by giving us the Torah.
We praise You, Lord,
Giver of the Torah.

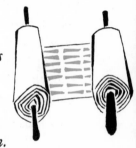

Amen.

THE CONGREGATION WILL SIT FOR THE READING OF THE TORAH

A. The Torah Reading
1. Based on Deuteronomy 29:9-14, 30:11-20.

You are standing this day, all of you, before your God: young and old, men, women, and children, your chiefs, and the stranger that is among you, to join into an agreement with Him. He will take you to Himself as His people, as He promised your fathers, Abraham, Isaac, and Jacob, and He will be your God, as you promised when you stood at the foot of Mt. Sinai. This agreement is not with you only, but with all the generations to come.

My commandment is not too hard for you, nor is it beyond your reach. Do not say, "Who will fly up to heaven to bring it back to us and teach us?" Do not say, "Who will go across the sea for us, to bring it back to us, and teach us?" No, my teaching is very near you, in your own mouth and in your own heart, and can be carried out.

See, I have set before you this day life and good, and death and evil . . . therefore choose life, that you may live, you and your children.

Love the Lord your God, walk in his ways, and keep his commandments. Then shall you live and enjoy the blessings of this land which I have given you. Heaven and earth are witnesses that I have set before you a choice between life and death, blessing and harm. Choose life, that you and your children may live, by loving the Lord your God, obeying His laws and holding Him close. This will give you a good life and a happy one, and you will live peacefully in your land.

2. Based on Leviticus 19:2-4, 9-18 (An Alternative Torah Reading for Yom Kippur).

You shall be holy, for I the Lord your God am holy. What does it mean to be holy? It means to live good lives, by keeping the laws of God. You shall show great respect to your mother and father. You shall keep the Sabbath. You shall not worship false gods. A farmer shall not gather up all his harvest, but shall leave a corner of his field for the poor and the stranger. You shall not steal, or cheat, or lie, or swear falsely. You shall remember God and keep to his ways. You shall not take advantage of your neighbor. When a man does work for you, you must pay his wages right away. You shall not insult a deaf person simply because he cannot hear, nor shall you put anything in the way of a blind man.

When you judge anyone, you must judge fairly. Do not be partial to the poor or favor the rich. Do not spread gossip about people, and do not stand around doing nothing when your neighbor is in trouble; I am the Lord.

Do not hate your brother in secret. If you are angry with him, talk to him about it, so that you may bring the trouble to an end. Never take revenge or bear a grudge against any of your people, but love your neighbor as yourself; I am the Lord.

READER

Baruch atta Adonai,	בָּרוּךְ אַתָּה יְיָ
elohaynu melech ha-olam,	אֱלֹהֵינוּ מֶלֶךְ הָעוֹלָם.
asher natan lanu Torat emet,	אֲשֶׁר נָתַן לָנוּ תּוֹרַת אֱמֶת.
v'cha-yay olam nata b'to-chaynu.	וְחַיֵּי עוֹלָם נָטַע בְּתוֹכֵנוּ.
Baruch atta Adonai,	בָּרוּךְ אַתָּה יְיָ.
notayn ha-Torah..	נוֹתֵן הַתּוֹרָה.

ALL READING

We praise You,
  O Lord our God, King of the universe,
  who have set eternal life within us
  by giving us a Torah of truth.
We praise You, Lord,
Giver of the Torah.

BLESSING BEFORE THE HAFTARAH

We praise You, Lord our God, King of the universe, for prophets of truth and justice. We praise You, Lord, the God of truth.

B. Haftarah

1. Based on Isaiah 57:14-58:14.

This is the word of God, who is holy, and who lives forever: I am in the high and holy places, the distant stars, and I am also with those who are modest and humble in spirit. I will not be angry for long. I bring healing and comfort to those who have been greedy, and who have angered me for a time. I am the God who brings peace to him that is near and to him that is far off, who gives spirit and life.

Why then do people do wrongly? Why do they call Me, pretending that they are doing the right thing? You complain because you have fasted and prayed, and yet have failed to please Me. But is fasting enough, when you still do wrong to your workers? Is fasting enough, when you continue to quarrel and fight? Such fasting will not make Me care for you. Is this the fast I have chosen? Is this the way you show that you are humble, and sorry for your wickedness? Do you think I am pleased simply because you come to Me with sad faces?

No, I have chosen another kind of fasting, another way of showing that you regret your wrongdoings: let those who are mistreated and enslaved go free, share your bread with the hungry, bring the homeless poor into your house. Give clothes to those who need them, do not pretend that you do not see them. Honor the Sabbath, keep the holy days. When you do such things, then you shall have light instead of darkness, joy instead of gloom. Then the Lord will be with you. You will be strong and well, like a garden which never lacks water, like a spring whose waters never fail. Your walls will be rebuilt, your streets renewed. You will live in peace and safety; I, the Lord, make you this promise.

2. Jonah (An Alternative Haftarah for Yom Kippur).

It happened that the Lord called to a man named Jonah, commanding him to bring a message to the people of a city called Nineveh, that they must change their evil ways before it was too late to save themselves. But Jonah did not wish to bring the message to those people, so he went to a ship going elsewhere, to Tarshish, and set sail on that ship, thinking that he could run away from God.

The ship had not been sailing very long when there was a mighty storm, and it was in danger of breaking up and sinking. The sailors were afraid. They threw things into the sea to lighten their vessel, and they prayed fearfully. Then they thought, "Perhaps our troubles are on account of someone who is aboard this ship." They cast lots to see upon whom it would fall, and Jonah was chosen. He told them his story.

"I am a Hebrew," he said, "and I worship the Lord, who made the heavens and the seas and the dry land. I thought I could escape him by taking this ship to a far-off place. Now we can see that I was foolish. Who can run away from God, who made all things and is everywhere?" The storm grew worse. And Jonah, knowing that the storm would not end until he was off the ship, advised the sailors to throw him overboard. They did not want to do this, but as there seemed to be no other way to abate the storm, Jonah was cast into the sea. The storm ended, and a great fish carried Jonah inside him for three days, until they reached the shore not far from Nineveh.

Once more the Lord's command came to the mind of Jonah. "Go to the city and give them my message." This time Jonah obeyed, for now he knew that near and far, the Lord rules all things. He came to Nineveh and cried out his warning: "Change your ways for the better before you are destroyed!"

The people listened and believed him. They regretted their wrongdoings. A proclamation of the king called on each citizen to turn from his evil ways and from violence. This was pleasing to God, and so, repenting, the people of Nineveh saved themselves.

But Jonah was not too pleased. He was annoyed that he had been sent to save this people. It angered him that the people had changed their ways and saved themselves, and that God, who loves all his children everywhere, showed them mercy. "I would rather have stayed at home," he thought. The word of God came again to his mind, saying, "Are you right to be angry, Jonah?"

Jonah was sitting a little way out at the edge of the city, thinking his thoughts and waiting to see what would happen. It was very hot, and he sat in the shade of a quick-growing plant, a gourd. Then the gourd withered, and the warm wind and hot sun made Jonah faint. "I wish I were dead," said Jonah. "This heat is killing me." And the word of God came to his mind once more, saying, "Are you sorry the plant died, Jonah?" "I surely am," thought Jonah. "Yes," said God, "you care about a plant which grew in a day and died in a day. And should I not care about Nineveh, a city with many thousands of repentant people and innocent beasts?"

THE CONGREGATION WILL STAND AS THE TORAH IS BROUGHT FORWARD

READER

גַּדְּלוּ לַיְיָ אִתִּי וּנְרוֹמְמָה שְׁמוֹ יַחְדָּו׃

Gaddelu l'Adonai iti, u-n'ro-m'mah shemo yach-dav.

O magnify the Lord with me,
    and let us exalt His name together.

CHOIR

Hodo al eretz v'shamayim	הוֹדוֹ עַל אֶרֶץ וְשָׁמָיִם׃
va-yarem keren l'ammo,	וַיָּרֶם קֶרֶן לְעַמּוֹ
t'hillah l'chol chasidav,	תְּהִלָּה לְכָל חֲסִידָיו
liv-nay yisrael,	לִבְנֵי יִשְׂרָאֵל
am k'rovo.	עַם קְרֹבוֹ
Halleluyah!	הַלְלוּיָהּ׃

His glory is over heaven and earth.
and He has raised His people high.
Let all who love Him praise Him.
Let the people Israel praise Him,
a people close to Him.
Praise the Lord!

READER
The law of the Lord is perfect, restoring the soul.

ALL READING
The teaching of the Lord is right,
rejoicing the heart.

READER
The commandment of the Lord is pure, enlightening the eyes.

ALL READING
The love of the Lord is strong,
lasting forever.

READER
A good teaching has been given you; keep it and live it. It is a tree of life to those who hold firmly to it, and those who cling to it are made happy. Its ways are ways of pleasantness, and all its paths are peace.

CHOIR

Etz chayyim hi	עֵץ חַיִּים הִיא
lammachazikim bah,	לַמַּחֲזִיקִים בָּהּ
v'tom'-chehah m'ushar.	וְתֹמְכֶיהָ מְאֻשָּׁר:
D'rachehah darchay noam,	דְּרָכֶיהָ דַרְכֵי נֹעַם
v'chol n'tivotehah	וְכָל נְתִיבוֹתֶיהָ
shalom.	שָׁלוֹם:
Hashivaynu Adonai	הֲשִׁיבֵנוּ יְיָ
aylecha v'nashuvah,	אֵלֶיךָ וְנָשׁוּבָה
chadaysh yamaynu k'kedem.	חַדֵּשׁ יָמֵינוּ כְּקֶדֶם:

THE ARK IS CLOSED
THE CONGREGATION WILL SIT
READER

Lord, we have learned through the study of Your Torah and through the history of our people many shining truths. May we never forget how good the world is, and how sweet is the taste of freedom. We know that our life and its goodness is the gift of loving parents and kind friends. And we know that their love and kindness are gifts from You, who are the Creator of all things.

ALL READING

Because we know all this, we know too that You created us, Your children, to live in peace and friendship all over the world. O let us all be filled with the spirit of wisdom and justice, love and mercy, that we may learn to make this a peaceful world. Then will there be enough for us all. No more shall any child go hungry, or any man be afraid, or any mother cry for her children lost in war. We praise You, Lord, Teacher of peace.

Now let us for a little while be very quiet. Let us hear only what our minds tell us, as we think about this day and of all that we have learned about ourselves, our God and the new year.

SILENT MEDITATION

CHOIR

May the words of my mouth	יִהְיוּ לְרָצוֹן אִמְרֵי פִי
and the meditations of my heart	וְהֶגְיוֹן לִבִּי
be acceptable in Your sight,	לְפָנֶיךָ
O Lord,	יְיָ
my Rock and my Redeemer.	צוּרִי וְגוֹאֲלִי:
Amen.	אָמֵן

THE CONGREGATION WILL STAND

ALL READING, OR ALL SINGING

Let us adore the ever-living God,
  and render praise unto Him
  Who spread out the heavens
  and established the earth,
  and whose glory
  is revealed in the heavens above
  and whose greatness
  is manifest throughout the world.
  He is our God and there is none else.

Va-anach-nu kor-im	וַאֲנַחְנוּ כֹּרְעִים
u-mish-ta-cha-vim u-mo-dim	וּמִשְׁתַּחֲוִים וּמוֹדִים
lif-nay melech	לִפְנֵי מֶלֶךְ
mal-chay ha-m'la-chim,	מַלְכֵי הַמְּלָכִים,
ha-ka-dosh baruch hu.	הַקָּדוֹשׁ, בָּרוּךְ הוּא.

75

READER

We bow the head in reverence, and worship the King of kings, the Holy One, praised be He.

We near the end of our service, and we call to mind another service. It was Yom Kippur, and a man brought his boy to the house of prayer.

ALL READING

He does not know the prayers,
he does not know the words,
He sits beside his father,
hearing words he does not know.

READER

All around him, the people chant, [their words and prayers are loud.] He sits beside his father, the holy words unsaid.

ALL READING

The morning prayers are ended,
the day is growing long,
His lips are silent still,
but his hands begin to move.

READER

In his hands appears a flute. He tugs at his father's sleeve. "Can I play my flute now, papa? I want to play my flute." His father's face is shocked. A flute in this holy place? No, this cannot be.

ALL READING

The afternoon service is done.
Now the prayers begin, called Ne'ilah,
when Jews try, through the power of their souls,
to open the gates of heaven,
before the day is done.

READER

Again the boy is heard. "I want to play my flute. Let me play it please." Again the father's impatient "no" returns to the pleading boy.

ALL READING

At last he cannot longer wait.
Flute leaps to mouth.
The air flies free.
The flute's singing voice is heard
    above the sound of prayer.

READER

His father is red with shame, and he takes the flute away. A little silence halts the prayer, and then the day goes on.

ALL READING

The shofar *is sounded,*
    deeper than any flute can be.
The holy Baal Shem Tov,
    Light of the World,
    approaches father and son.

READER

What will he say? Will angry words come from his holy mouth? Has this day's prayer been wasted? Will anger now be its end?

ALL READING

The saintly Rabbi speaks:
"Thank you!
You blew that flute with all your heart!
Your prayer was truer than any of ours."

READER

And more than that: "It is the heart that prays—far more than the words we utter with our lips. May every child of Israel be filled with such love as yours. You have this day lifted all our prayers to heaven on the wings of your spirit."

READER

Let us once more, as we hope that the New Year will bring goodness for us all, say to each other the ancient words of blessing:

ALL SINGING

Eli, Eli	אֵלִי, אֵלִי,
shelo yi-ga-mer l'olam,	שֶׁלֹּא יִגָּמֵר לְעוֹלָם
ha-chol v'ha-yam,	הַחוֹל וְהַיָּם,
rish-rush shel ha-ma-yim,	רִשְׁרוּשׁ שֶׁל הַמַּיִם,
b'rak ha-sha-ma-yim,	בְּרַק הַשָּׁמַיִם,
t'fi-lat ha-a-dam.	תְּפִלַּת הָאָדָם.
ha-chol v'ha-yam,	הַחוֹל וְהַיָּם,
rish-rush shel ha-ma-yim,	רִשְׁרוּשׁ שֶׁל הַמַּיִם,
b'rak ha-sha-ma-yim,	בְּרַק הַשָּׁמַיִם,
t'fi-lat ha-a-dam.	תְּפִלַּת הָאָדָם.

O Lord, my God,
I pray that these things never end:

The sand and the sea,
The rush of the waters,
The crash of the heavens,
The prayer of man.
The sand and the sea,
The rush of the waters,
The crash of the heavens,
The prayer of man.

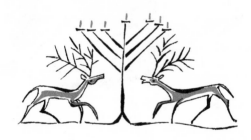

READER

Let us once more, as we hope that the New Year will bring goodness for us all, say to each other the ancient words of blessing:

ALL READING

לְשָׁנָה טוֹבָה תִּכָּתֵבוּ וְתֵחָתֵמוּ:

L'shana tovah ti-ka-tay-vu v'tay-cha-tay-mu.

"May you be written down
and sealed for a good year."

ADDITIONAL READINGS FOR
ROSH HASHANAH AND YOM KIPPUR

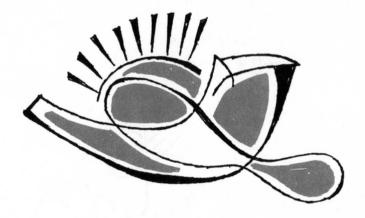

1. EVERYONE SANG

Everyone suddenly burst out singing;
And I was filled with such delight
As prisoned birds must find in freedom,
Winging wildly across the white
Orchards and dark-green fields;
    on—on—and out of sight.
Everyone's voice was suddenly lifted;
And beauty came like the setting sun;
My heart was shaken with tears; and horror
Drifted away . . . Oh, but everyone
Was a bird; and the song was wordless—
    the singing will never be done.

                              —Siegfried Sassoon

2. LORD, WE ASK FOR THIS

Lord, be with all who are today alone and lonely;
Let them know that they have a Friend.
Lord, hear those who speak without being heard,
Let them know that there is One who understands them.
Lord, heal those who are in pain, who are weak and tired;
Let them know that they will be well and strong
    in days to come.
Lord, take all those who are afraid and give them hope;
Take those who have been hurt by word or hand
    and teach them not to hate.
Lord, teach us to love one another.
Give us strength to make this world a place of peace
    and mercy and justice.
Lord, give us the knowledge that You are with us
    and in us,
Whenever men work for a better life.

                              —C. S.

3.　　*Avinu mal-key-nu, Our Father, our King*

READER, THEN CONGREGATION

Avinu mal-kay-nu,　אָבִינוּ מַלְכֵּנוּ,

Our Father, our King
we have sinned, we have done wrong.

Avinu mal-kay-nu,　אָבִינוּ מַלְכֵּנוּ,

Our Father, our King
write our names in the book of forgiveness.

Avinu mal-kay-nu,　אָבִינוּ מַלְכֵּנוּ,

Our Father, our King
write our names in the Book of Life.

Avinu mal-kay-nu,　אָבִינוּ מַלְכֵּנוּ,

Our Father, our King
may the coming year be a happy one for all of us.

Avinu mal-kay-nu,　אָבִינוּ מַלְכֵּנוּ,

Our Father, our King
fill our hands with Your blessings.

Avinu mal-kay-nu,　אָבִינוּ מַלְכֵּנוּ,

Our Father, our King
let no one plan to harm us in the year ahead.

Avinu mal-kay-nu,　אָבִינוּ מַלְכֵּנוּ,

Our Father, our King
let us be free of anger, hate and jealousy
during the year to come.

Avinu mal-kay-nu, אָבִינוּ מַלְכֵּנוּ,
Our Father, our King
  give strength and peace to Your people Israel.

Avinu mal-kay-nu, אָבִינוּ מַלְכֵּנוּ,
Our Father, our King
  fill us with love for Israel, our people.

Avinu mal-kay-nu, אָבִינוּ מַלְכֵּנוּ,
Our Father, our King
  strengthen our love for all people, of every
  color and nation.

Avinu mal-kay-nu, אָבִינוּ מַלְכֵּנוּ,
Our Father, our King
  open the gates of heaven to our prayers.

Avinu mal-kay-nu, אָבִינוּ מַלְכֵּנוּ,
Our Father, our King
  be kind to us and answer us, even if our
  good deeds are few.
Treat us with charity and kindness, and help us.

4. MY THREAD

To the new wick
Of freedom's torch,
Oh world,
I, travel-stained,
With my wanderer's stick
And this ancient pain of mine,
I, too, have brought
A white linen thread
Dipped in red wine
For the new wick
Of freedom's torch,
That with thread of all colors
Is woven thick.
When it burns, and the red
With smoke is black,
I shall not know
Which is my thread.
But for me the thought
Will be enough,
That I too brought
My thread for the new wick
Of freedom's torch,
Oh world!

—David Hofstein

5. WHAT CAN I DO?

What can I do?
I can talk out when others are silent.
I can say man when others say money.
I can stay up when others are asleep.
I can keep on working
    when others have stopped to play.
I can give life big meanings
    when others give life little meanings.
I can say love when others say hate.
I can say every man
    when others say one man.
I can try events by a hard test
    when others try it by an easy test.
What can I do?
I can give myself to life
    when other men refuse themselves to life.

                                —*Horace Traubel*

6. DREAMS

Hold fast to dreams
For if dreams die
Life is a broken-winged bird
That cannot fly.
Hold fast to dreams
For when dreams go
Life is a barren field
Frozen with snow.

                                 —*Langston Hughes*

7. A MINOR BIRD

I have wished a bird would fly away,
And not sing by my house all day;
Have clapped my hands at him from the door
When it seemed as if I could bear no more.
The fault must partly have been in me.
The bird was not to blame for his key.
And of course there must be something wrong
In wanting to silence any song.

—*Robert Frost*

8. O LORD, OUR LORD

O Lord, our Lord,
Your glory is known on all the earth.
Even the song of children flies higher than the heavens
*   to tell of Your greatness.*
I look at the sky, made by Your fingers,
The moon and the stars, the work of Your hands,
*   and I wonder:*
What is man, that You think of him,
What are we, that You care for us?
Yet You have made us only a little less than angels,
You have crowned us with glory and honor.
And You have put all things in our care:
Sheep and oxen,
The beasts of the field,
The birds of the air,
The fish of the sea,
Whatever swims through the currents of the deep.
O Lord, our Lord,
Your glory is known in all the earth.

Based on Psalm 148

9. PRAISE THE LORD!

Praise the Lord!
Praise Him in the heavens,
Praise Him in far space.
Let all His angels praise Him;
Praise Him, O sun and moon.
Praise Him, all you stars of light,
Praise Him, all that is.
Praise Him, sing to Him,
Let the happy shout be heard.
Shark and whale, fire and hail,
Snow and frost, wind and storm—praise Him!
Mountain and field,
Apple tree and oak—praise Him!
Lion and cow,
Eagle and ant—praise Him!
Kings and chiefs,
Young and old—praise Him!
His glory is higher than heaven,
Yet He is very near—
As near as the heart that beats out love,
And the lips that sing Him praise.
Halleluyah—Praise the Lord!

—*Based on Psalm 148*

10. HOW BEAUTIFUL UPON THE MOUNTAINS

How beautiful upon the mountains
Are the feet of him who brings good tidings,
Who announces news of peace, the bringer of good news
Who brings news of freedom;
Who says to Zion: "Your God is King."
Hear the watchmen cry out!
They lift up their voices and together
Face to face they sing for joy,
That God has returned to Zion.
O Jerusalem that was in ruins,
Be joyful, and break into song together,
For God is comforting His people,
And Jerusalem is free again.
The Lord has shown His power,
And all the nations have seen it.
And God shall bring freedom
To all the ends of earth.

—Based on Isaiah 52:7-10

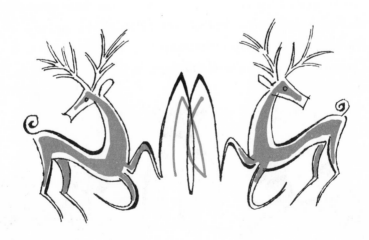

11. THE PRAYER OF JONAH

Lord, You tossed me down into the deep waters,
Into the heart of the seas.
(I thought I could run away.)
The waves and billows passed far over me,
And I said: I have been cast out,
Will I ever be close to You again?
(I couldn't be bothered for the sake of others.)
The waters pressed around me, as
I went deep down, deep, to darkness and silence,
To the foot of the mountains of the sea—
The weeds were wrapped about my head.
And I never thought to see land again, I saw
The earth with her bars closed over me forever.
(You sent me to save a city, but I ran away.)
But You brought me out of the ocean grave;
Fainting with fear I called to You,
I prayed with a full heart,
And You listened.
(Now send me to save Your children. I am ready to go.)
So Jonah went to Nineveh, a great city,
And brought its people the word of God:
Change your evil ways, learn to do good,
*   and you will be saved.*
If you do not, then beware, for your doom
*   will not be long delayed.*
And the people heard, and listened, and changed,
And there was joy in heaven and upon the earth.
Instead of destruction there was peace, and singing.

Based on Jonah 2:3

12. LOVE FOR MY PEOPLE

I know a flower that grows and blooms
Without dew or rain.
It has no need of sun and wind,
It thrives in gloom and pain.
It grows in storms and snow,
When all flowers die.
The storm gives it strength and sap,
Fragrance and brilliancy.
When thunder and lightning crash,
And great trees fall,
It lifts its head, refreshed and bright,
Radiant over all.
The flower is love of my people.
It blossoms in the storm.
It draws its sap from suffering,
And the cold blast keeps it warm.

—Yehoash

13. THE BRIDGE

I am the bridge.
Over my neck
The people pass from shore to shore,
To the happy days in store.
I am the bridge. I hang
Over chasms deep as hell.
I see what lies below,
But I never tell.
I am the bridge. Endlessly,

The people pass over me
To the land of joy and might.
And day and night,
Night and day,
God, this is my prayer,
Give me strength,
That their weight I can bear.

—Yehoash

14. HANDS
The song of hands is the song of God,
Though none have seen God's hand,
The hand of the Lord that created all—
The sky and the sea and the land.
When hands are at work doing things,
Creation sings—something done!
The breath of the world rejoices to see
Hands working with wood and stone.
Hands make windows to catch the sun,
And dams to hold waters back.
And hands make lamps, that send out light,
Though the night is black.

—Ezekiel Brownstone

ADDITIONAL SONGS FOR ROSH HASHANAH
AND YOM KIPPUR

ADON OLAM

Adon olam asher malach	אֲדוֹן עוֹלָם אֲשֶׁר מָלַךְ
b'terem kol y'tzir nivra	בְּטֶרֶם כָּל יְצִיר נִבְרָא:
l'et na'a-sah, v'chef-tzo kol	לְעֵת נַעֲשָׂה בְחֶפְצוֹ כֹּל
azai melech, sh'mo nikra.	אֲזַי מֶלֶךְ שְׁמוֹ נִקְרָא.
V'a-charay kich-lot ha-kol	וְאַחֲרֵי כִּכְלוֹת הַכֹּל
l'va-do yim-loch no-ra	לְבַדּוֹ יִמְלוֹךְ נוֹרָא.
v'hu ha-ya, v'hu ho-veh	וְהוּא הָיָה וְהוּא הֹוֶה
v'hu yi-yeh, b'tif-arah.	וְהוּא יִהְיֶה בְּתִפְאָרָה.
V'hu echad, v'ayn shay-ni	וְהוּא אֶחָד וְאֵין שֵׁנִי
l'ham-shil lo, l'hach-birah	לְהַמְשִׁיל לוֹ לְהַחְבִּירָה.
b'li ray-sheet, b'li tach-leet	בְּלִי רֵאשִׁית בְּלִי תַכְלִית
v'lo ha-oz, v'ha-mis-rah.	וְלוֹ הָעֹז וְהַמִּשְׂרָה.
V'hu ay-li, v'chai go-a-li	וְהוּא אֵלִי וְחַי גּוֹאֲלִי
v'tzur chev-li, b'ayt tza-rah	וְצוּר חֶבְלִי בְּעֵת צָרָה.
v'hu ni-si u-ma-nos li	וְהוּא נִסִּי וּמָנוֹס לִי
m'nat ko-si, b'yom ek-ra.	מְנָת כּוֹסִי בְּיוֹם אֶקְרָא.
B'ya-do af-kid ru-chi	בְּיָדוֹ אַפְקִיד רוּחִי
b'ayt i-shan v'a-ira	בְּעֵת אִישַׁן וְאָעִירָה.
v'im ru-chi g'vi-ya-ti	וְעִם רוּחִי גְּוִיָּתִי
Adonai li, v'lo i-ra.	יְיָ לִי וְלֹא אִירָא.

Lord of all, You ruled the world
  before any creature raised its head.
When all was made to Your command
Your name was King, as You had planned.
And when all things have passed away,
You still as King shall rule the day
You were, and are, and shall remain.
Forever Your glory shall men exclaim.
You are One. No other gods are there
To join with You or Your greatness share.
Without beginning, without an end,
Yours is the power, Yours the throne.
You are my God, my living shield,
  my rock of help when trouble comes.
To You I run, Your flag I lift
You are with me, on the day I call.
In Your hands my soul You keep.
  when I wake and when I sleep.
My body too, along with soul—
The Lord is with me, I do not fear.

LO YISA GOY

Lo yisa goy el goy cherev

Lo yil-m'du od mil-cha-ma.

לֹא־יִשָּׂא גוֹי אֶל־גּוֹי חֶרֶב

לֹא־יִלְמְדוּ עוֹד מִלְחָמָה:

Nation shall not lift up sword against nation,
They shall study war no more.

CHORUS
HALLELUHU

Halle-lu-hu, hallelu-yah,	הַלְלוּהוּ, הַלְלוּיָהּ
b'tzil-tze-lay sha-ma,	בְּצִלְצְלֵי שָׁמַע,
Halle-lu-hu, hallelu-yah,	הַלְלוּהוּ, הַלְלוּיָהּ
b'tzil-tze-lay t'ru-ah,	בְּצִלְצְלֵי תְרוּעָה,
Kol ha-n'sha-ma t'hallel yah,	כֹּל הַנְּשָׁמָה תְּהַלֵּל יָהּ,
hallelu-ya, hallelu-yah	הַלְלוּיָהּ (2).
Kol ha-n'sha-ma t'hallel yah,	כֹּל הַנְּשָׁמָה תְּהַלֵּל יָהּ,
hallelu-ya, hallelu-yah.	הַלְלוּיָהּ (2).

Praise Him, praise, with trumpet and drum,
With strings and winds and voice,
Praise Him, praise, with song and with prayer,
With joy, with dance and with love.
Let all who breathe sing praise to the Lord,
Hallelu-yah, hallelu-yah,
Let all who breathe sing praise to the Lord,
Hallelu-yah, hallelu-yah.

SHOMER YISRAEL

Shomer, shomer Yisrael	שׁוֹמֵר, שׁוֹמֵר יִשְׂרָאֵל,
Sh'mor sh'ay-rit Yisrael	שְׁמֹר שְׁאֵרִית יִשְׂרָאֵל,
Shomer, shomer Yisrael	שׁוֹמֵר, שׁוֹמֵר יִשְׂרָאֵל,
Sh'mor sh'ay-rit Yisrael.	שְׁמֹר שְׁאֵרִית יִשְׂרָאֵל,
V'al yo-vad,	וְאַל יֹאבַד,
v'al yo-vad Yisrael,	וְאַל יֹאבַד יִשְׂרָאֵל,

V'al yo-vad, v'al yo-vad Yisrael, וְאַל יֹאבַד, וְאַל יֹאבַד יִשְׂרָאֵל,

ha-o-m'rim, ha-o-m'rim, הָאוֹמְרִים, הָאוֹמְרִים,

ha-o-m'rim "Shema Yisrael." הָאוֹמְרִים שְׁמַע יִשְׂרָאֵל!

Shomer, shomer goy echad, שׁוֹמֵר, שׁוֹמֵר גּוֹי אֶחָד,

sh'mor sh'ay-rit am echad. שְׁמֹר שְׁאֵרִית עַם אֶחָד,

Shomer, shomer goy echad, שׁוֹמֵר, שׁוֹמֵר גּוֹי אֶחָד,

sh'mor sh'ay-rit am echad. שְׁמֹר שְׁאֵרִית עַם אֶחָד,

V'al yo-vad, v'al yo-vad וְאַל יֹאבַד, וְאַל יֹאבַד

goy echad גּוֹי אֶחָד

V'al yo-vad, v'al yo-vad וְאַל יֹאבַד, וְאַל יֹאבַד

goy echad גּוֹי אֶחָד

ha-m'ya-cha-dim, ha-m'ya-cha-dim הַמְיַחֲדִים, הַמְיַחֲדִים,

shim-cha Adonai echad. שִׁמְךָ, אֲדֹנָי אֶחָד!

O Guardian of Israel
Protect our scattered people.
Let not Israel be lost,
The faithful people,
Who never tire of saying:
"Hear, O Israel."
O Guardian of this chosen people
Protect our remaining brothers.
Let us not be lost,
Who call you One.
Forever saying:
"The Lord is One."

95

MI-PI EL

Ayn adir k'Adonai,	אֵין אַדִּיר כַּאדֹנָי,
V'ayn baruch k'ven Amram.	וְאֵין בָּרוּךְ כְּבֶן עַמְרָם.
Ayan g'do-lah ka-Torah,	אֵין גְּדוֹלָה כַּתּוֹרָה,
V'ayn d'gulim k'Yisrael.	וְאֵין דְּגוּלִים כְּיִשְׂרָאֵל.
Mi-pi El (2) yit-ba-rach Yisrael.	מִפִּי אֵל (2) יִתְבָּרֵךְ יִשְׂרָאֵל.

Ayn hadur k'Adonai,	אֵין הָדוּר כַּאדֹנָי.
V'ayn vatik k'ven Amram.	וְאֵין וָתִיק כְּבֶן עַמְרָם.
Ayn za-kah ka-Torah,	אֵין זַכָּה כַּתּוֹרָה,
V'ayn chasidim k'Yisrael.	וְאֵין חֲסִידִים כְּיִשְׂרָאֵל.

Mi-pi El (2) yit-ba-rach Yisrael.	מִפִּי אֵל (2) יִתְבָּרֵךְ יִשְׂרָאֵל.
Ayn ta-hor k'Adonai	אֵין טָהוֹר כַּאדֹנָי,
V'ayn ya-chid k'ven Amram	וְאֵין יָחִיד כְּבֶן עַמְרָם.
Ayn ka-bi-rah ka-Torah,	אֵין כַּבִּירָה כַּתּוֹרָה,
V'ayn lam-da-nim k'Yisrael.	וְאֵין לַמְדָנִים כְּיִשְׂרָאֵל.
Mi-pi El (2) yit-ba-rach Yisrael.	מִפִּי אֵל (2) יִתְבָּרֵךְ יִשְׂרָאֵל.
Mi-pi El (2) yit-ba-rach Yisrael.	מִפִּי אֵל (2) יִתְבָּרֵךְ יִשְׂרָאֵל.

There is none Almighty as the Lord
And none so Blessed as Moses was
Nothing so Choice as Torah's words
And none so Devoted as Israel.

God's voice, God's voice—
May it bless all Israel.

There is none so Exalted as the Lord
And none more Famous than Moses is
Nothing Greater than Torah's truth
And none more Happy than Israel is.

There is none who is Infinite as is the Lord
And none so Just as Moses was
Nothing so Kind as Torah laws
And none more Learned than Israel is.

ESA EYNAI

Esa ay-nai, el heh-ha-rim,	אֶשָּׂא עֵינַי אֶל הֶהָרִים,
may-a-yin ya-vo, ya-vo ez-ri?	מֵאַיִן יָבֹא עֶזְרִי?
Esa ay-nai, el heh-ha-rim,	אֶשָּׂא עֵינַי אֶל הֶהָרִים,
may-a-yin ya-vo, ya-vo ez-ri.	מֵאַיִן יָבֹא עֶזְרִי?
Ez-ri may-im Adonai,	עֶזְרִי מֵעִם יְיָ,
O-seh sha-ma-yim va-a-retz	עֹשֵׂה שָׁמַיִם וָאָרֶץ.
Ez-ri may-im Adonai,	עֶזְרִי מֵעִם יְיָ,
O-seh sha-ma-yim va-a-retz.	עֹשֵׂה שָׁמַיִם וָאָרֶץ.

I lift up mine eyes, unto the mountains,
From whence, from whence shall my help come?
I lift up mine eyes, unto the mountains,
From whence, from whence shall my help come?
My help will come from the Lord,
Maker of heaven and earth.
My help will come from the Lord,
Maker of heaven and earth.

IM EYN ANI LI

Im ayn ani li, mi li,

u-ch'sheh-a-ni l'atz'mi   mah a'ni

v'im lo ach-shav ay-ma-tai, ay-ma-tai.

אִם אֵין אֲנִי לִי מִי לִי,

וּכְשֶׁאֲנִי לְעַצְמִי מָה אֲנִי,

וְאִם לֹא עַכְשָׁו

אֵימָתַי, אֵימָתָי.

If I am not for myself, who will be?
If I am only for myself, what am I?
If not now, when? when?

EMET

Emet, emet, emet, emet,	אֱמֶת, אֱמֶת, אֱמֶת, אֱמֶת,
Emet, emet, emet, emet,	אֱמֶת, אֱמֶת, אֱמֶת, אֱמֶת,
Emet atta hu ri-shon;	אֱמֶת אַתָּה הוּא רִאשׁוֹן,
Emet, emet, emet, emet,	אֱמֶת, אֱמֶת, אֱמֶת, אֱמֶת,
Emet, emet, emet, emet,	אֱמֶת, אֱמֶת, אֱמֶת, אֱמֶת,
Emet atta hu a-cha-ron.	אֱמֶת אַתָּה הוּא אַחֲרוֹן
U-mi-bal-a-de-cha, ayn la-nu melech,	וּמִבַּלְעָדֶיךָ אֵין לָנוּ מֶלֶךְ,
Go-ayl u-mo-shi-a;	גּוֹאֵל וּמוֹשִׁיעַ.
U-mi-bal-a-de-cha, ayn la-nu melech,	וּמִבַּלְעָדֶיךָ אֵין לָנוּ מֶלֶךְ,
Go-ayl u-mo-shi-a.	גּוֹאֵל וּמוֹשִׁיעַ.

Emet ...
Emet ...
True it is, that You are the First;
Emet ...
Emet ...
True it is, that You are the Last.
And without You, we have no King,
Helper or Friend;
And without You, we have no King,
Helper or Friend.

DONA DONA

On a wagon, bound for market,
There's a calf with a mournful cry.
High above him, there's a swallow
Winging swiftly through the sky.

CHORUS

How the winds are laughing!
They laugh with all their might.
Laugh and laugh the whole day through
And half the summer's night.
Dona, dona, dona, dona,
Dona, dona, dona, dai.
Dona, dona, dona, dona,
Dona, dona, dona, dai.

Stop complaining, said the farmer,
Who told you a calf to be?
Why don't you have wings to fly with
Like the swallow so brave and free?

CHORUS

Calves are easily bound and slaughtered,
Never knowing the reason why.
But whoever treasures freedom
Like the swallow has learned to fly.

CHORUS

NO MAN IS AN ISLAND

No man is an island, no man stands alone.
Each man's joy is joy to me.
Each man's grief is my own.
We need one another, so I will defend,
Each man as my brother, each man as my friend.
I saw the people gather, I heard the music start.
The song that they were singing,
Is ringing in my heart.

No man is an island, no man stands alone.
Each man's joy is joy to me.
Each man's grief is my own.
We need one another, so I will defend,
Each man as my brother, each man as my friend.

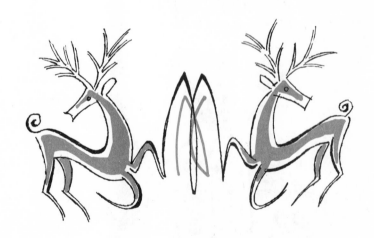

Avinu mal-kay-nu,   אָבִינוּ מַלְכֵּנוּ

    cha-nay-nu va-a-nay-nu,   חָנֵּנוּ וַעֲנֵנוּ

    avinu mal-kay-nu,   אָבִינוּ מַלְכֵּנוּ

    cha-nay-nu va-a-nay-nu,   חָנֵּנוּ וַעֲנֵנוּ

    ki ayn ba-nu ma-a-sim.   כִּי אֵין בָּנוּ מַעֲשִׂים

A-say i-ma-nu,   עֲשֵׂה עִמָּנוּ

    tze-da-kah va-che-sed,   צְדָקָה וָחֶסֶד

    a-say i-ma-nu,   עֲשֵׂה עִמָּנוּ

    tze-da-kah va-che-sed,   צְדָקָה וָחֶסֶד

    v'ho-shi-ay-nu.   וְהוֹשִׁיעֵנוּ:

Our Father, our King,
*   be kind to us and answer us,*
*   even if our good deeds are few.*
Treat us with charity and kindness,
*   and help us.*

NOTES AND ACKNOWLEDGMENTS

All new prayers have been written by Rabbi Chaim Stern. Traditional liturgical and biblical passages are not specially noted. Translations of such passages are by Rabbi Stern. The purpose of the following is to acknowledge copyrighted poems, songs and prayers. Every effort has been made to trace copyrighted materials used in this volume. If there is any copyrighted material which has not been acknowledged, its inclusion was inadvertant.

POEMS AND PRAYERS

1. *Grant us peace* . . . Very freely adapted by C. S. from the Union Prayerbook, Newly Revised, Part I, ©. C.C.A.R., 1940, p. 22. Used by permission.

2. *Let us adore* . . . From Union Prayerbook, p. 71, used by permission.

3. *Three things there are* . . . Paraphrased by Louis Untermeyer from the Persian, in the *Golden Treasury of Poetry,* Selected and with A Commentary by Louis Untermeyer, p. 306. Copyright The Golden Press, Inc.

4. *Everyone Sang* . . . by Siegfried Sassoon. From *Collected Poems* by Siegfried Sassoon. Copyright 1920 by E. P. Dutton & Company, renewed 1948 by Siegfried Sassoon. Reprinted by permission of The Viking Press, Inc.

5. *My Thread* . . . by David Hofstein
Love for My People . . . by Yehoash
The Bridge . . . by Yehoash
Hands . . . by Ezekiel Brownstone

The four poems above are from *The Golden Peacock,* Compiled, Translated and Edited by Joseph Leftwich. Reprinted by permission of A. S. Barnes & Company, Inc., including publications of Thomas Yoseloff. Copyright 1961.

6. *A Minor Bird* . . . by Robert Frost. From *The Poetry of Robert Frost* edited by Edward Connery Lathem. Copyright 1928 by Holt, Rinehart and Winston, Inc. Copyright © 1956 by Robert Frost. Reprinted by permission of Holt, Rinehart and Winston, Inc.

7. *Dreams* . . . by Langston Hughes. Copyright 1932 and renewed 1960 by Langston Hughes. Reprinted from *The Dream Keeper,* by Langston Hughes, by permission of Alfred A. Knopf, Inc.

In addition to the above, we note several poems not subject to copyright. *Who Has Seen the Wind? . . .* The first two stanzas are by Christina Rossetti; the additional ones are by C. S. *What Can I Do? . . .* by Horace Traubel.

SONGS

1. *Eli Eli . . .* There is a musical setting to the (Hebrew) words of Hannah Senesch by D. Zahavi.

2. *Eyn Keyloheynu . . .* We recommend the setting by B. Belfer, published by Transcontinental Music Publications, c. 1957.

3. *Esa Eynai . . .* We recommend the setting to this excerpt from Psalm 121 by Shlomo Carlebach.

4. *No Man Is An Island . . .* The words and music are by Joan Whitney and Alex Kramer. c. 1950, Bourne Co., New York, N.Y. Used by permission of the authors and copyright owner.

5. *Dona, Dona . . .* Yiddish lyric by Aaron Zeitlin, English lyric by Sheldon Secunda, Teddi Schwartz and Arthur Kevess. Music by Sholom Secunda. Copyright 1940·by Mills Music, Inc., New York, N.Y. Copyright © renewed 1968 by Mills Music, Inc., New York, N.Y. Copyright © 1956 by Mills Music, Inc., New York, N.Y.

The settings for the other musical passages in this volume are various and well-known. We do, however, wish to recommend such sources as *The Songs We Sing,* by H. Coopersmith; *Manginoth Shireynu,* by M. Nathanson; *The Union Songster; The Jewish Center Songster;* Transcontinental Music Publications; and *Songs of Our People,* by S. Bugatch. Readers will doubtless think of additional sources, such as the publication of the United Synagogue of America, the collections edited by Judith Eisenberg, and the growing collection of Chassidic music now being made available. In addition to "straight" liturgical music, we have included several contemporary "folk" songs. This type of music, including "folk rock," can be a valuable resource, when used judiciously, and the songs included are intended as a sample only. Modern Hebrew and Israeli songs constitute another very rich resource. Some of these are collected in the NFTY Songster, as well as in other collections, but a really thorough collection, with words and music, still awaits publication.